# OBLOMOV

Borgo Press Dramas by FRANK J. MORLOCK

*Chuzzlewit*
*Crime and Punishment*
*Falstaff* (with William Shakespeare, John Dennis, and William Kendrick)
*Fathers and Sons*
*Justine*
*Notes from the Underground*
*Oblomov*
*Outrageous Women: Lady Macbeth and Other French Plays* (editor and translator)
*The Princess Casamassima*
*A Raw Youth*
*The Stendhal Hamlet Scenarios and Other Shakespearean Shorts from the French* (editor and translator)
*Under Western Eyes*

# OBLOMOV
## A PLAY IN THREE ACTS

# FRANK J. MORLOCK

Adapted from the Novel by Ivan Goncharov

THE BORGO PRESS
MMXII

OBLOMOV

Copyright © 2012 by Frank J. Morlock

FIRST EDITION

Published by Wildside Press LLC

www.wildsidebooks.com

# DEDICATION

*For my son, Miles Stanton Morlock*

# CONTENTS

| | |
|---|---|
| CAST OF CHARACTERS | 9 |
| ACT I, Scene 1 | 11 |
| ACT II, Scene 2 | 86 |
| ACT II, Scene 3 | 100 |
| ACT II, Scene 4 | 116 |
| ACT III, Scene 5 | 155 |
| ACT III, Scene 6 | 181 |
| ACT III, Scene 7 | 200 |
| ABOUT THE AUTHOR | 213 |

# CAST OF CHARACTERS

Oblomov, around thirty years of age

Zakhar, an old serf about fifty years of age

Alekseyev, a well-dressed man about Oblomov's age

Stolz, a vigorous man of about thirty

Tarantyev, a large, overbearing man

Olga Sergeyevna, a handsome woman, a few years older than Oblomov

Madame Pshenitsyn, "Katrinka," a doll-like woman, with very little intellect, but an excellent housekeeper and mother

**Note**: In the nineteenth century the term "Oblomovism" passed into the vocabulary to describe a kind of helpless nobleman who couldn't "do" anything but live a life of torpor.

The action takes place in nineteenth-century Russia.

# ACT I
## SCENE 1: St. Petersburg, the First of May

*Oblomov's bedroom, late morning. To the audience's left, a large four-poster bed in which Oblomov is blissfully sleeping. To the far left, a door leading to the street. To the right of the bed, against the far wall, a desk. To the right, a door leading into the rest of the house. A couch and table to the right of the bed. The house is quiet. Oblomov stirs, stretches, and to his surprise finds himself fully awake. He starts to rise, even putting one foot out of bed, then, as if shocked by his own temerity, pulls it back again. Cautiously, he begins to move again.*

**Oblomov**

Enough of this! Time to get to work. It's almost noon. (despite these vigorous words, Oblomov barely stirs) Now or never, as Stolz would say. (with great effort he sits up) Yahh! (yawning) If only Stolz were here. (lies back down) It's still early. (pause) Zakhar! (pause) Zakhar! (irritated, he sits up) Now where is that lazy fellow...? I have to do everything myself! (he puts a naked foot out, touching the cold floor, and recoils, trembling) Zakhar! Zakhar!

(Entering from the right is an old serf. Not particularly lazy, but by no means a bundle of energy. He is dressed rather shabbily. He has taken care of Oblomov since Oblomov was a child.

Zakhar is irascible, as any man would be who has spent most of his adult life waiting on a child, but it is obvious that he retains affection for Oblomov.)

**Zakhar**

(grumbling) Zakhar, Zakhar, Zakhar! That's all I ever hear. For thirty years! When will he ever learn to do anything for himself like other people? (to Oblomov) Well? What do you want now?

**Oblomov**

(shrieking) My slippers! You know I can't get out of bed without my slippers.

**Zakhar**

Your slippers?

**Oblomov**

My slippers. What have you done with them this time?

**Zakhar**

Me? Done with your slippers?

**Oblomov**

Yes, you. You always do this to me.

**Zakhar**

I never touched your slippers. You had them on last night.

**Oblomov**

That's what you always say. No more excuses.

**Zakhar**

Hmm.

**Oblomov**

Don't just stand there...find them!

**Zakhar**

O Lord—when will my sufferings cease? (spotting the slippers under the bed) There they are!

**Oblomov**

Where?

**Zakhar**

Right there. You kicked them under the bed.

**Oblomov**

Well, put them on for me, can't you? You're preventing me from getting out of bed.

**Zakhar**

Couldn't you do that yourself?

**Oblomov**

So! You're being impudent again.

**Zakhar**

Impudent! Me?

**Oblomov**

Yes, you. You know very well your job is to take care of me.

**Zakhar**

I suppose you couldn't do it?

**Oblomov**

(innocently) Of course not. You know very well, I can't do anything by myself.

**Zakhar**

Oh, very well. Here. (putting on Oblomov's slippers)

**Oblomov**

Thank you. Next time, mind where you put them.

**Zakhar**

Argghh!

**Oblomov**

I really don't know how I put up with your laziness. You're

lucky I'm good natured.

**Zakhar**

Do you want to eat now?

**Oblomov**

Not yet. I haven't bathed yet. I always bathe before I eat.

**Zakhar**

You mean, I always take a bath for you before I feed you. Do you want your bath, then?

**Oblomov**

(considering, it's a difficult decision) Hmm. It's still a little early. But, I'm getting hungry and I have to bathe before I eat, hmm. What shall I do? (pause) Well?

**Zakhar**

Well, what?

**Oblomov**

Do I have to tell you every time? Can't you remember anything? I'll bathe.

**Zakhar**

(furious) Oh, very well.

(Oblomov begins to remove his long, flowing Persian gown, while Zakhar places a screen in front of him. Zakhar goes out and returns with a portable tub.)

**Oblomov**

I don't understand why Zakhar is so lazy, so slow in doing the simplest thing. It's beyond me how anybody can be like that. Brr! It's cold. (puts his robe back on)

**Zakhar**

Get in.

**Oblomov**

But, there's no water.

**Zakhar**

Get in, and I'll put the water in.

**Oblomov**

Put the water in first then, I'll get in.

**Zakhar**

O Lord! (goes out and returns with several buckets of water which are splashing all over the place) Now, get in.

**Oblomov**

Wait! I have to take off my robe.

**Zakhar**

All right.

**Oblomov**

Aiee! This water is too hot!

**Zakhar**

I'll fix that. (more splashing)

**Oblomov**

That's better. (Zakhar starts to leave) Where are you going?

**Zakhar**

What's the use of standing here while you're bathing?

**Oblomov**

Don't leave me alone. You always want to leave me alone. Can't you wait a little?

**Zakhar**

All right. I'll wait.

**Oblomov**

Where did you put that letter I received yesterday? Scrub my back.

**Zakhar**

What letter?

**Oblomov**

The one you gave me. To the left a little. Ahh—

**Zakhar**

I gave it to you? How should I know what you did with it?

**Oblomov**

(petulantly) You never know anything. Look behind the sofa. Just look at that sofa. Still unrepaired. Why don't you have it fixed? Aiee! Don't scrub so hard. Go look for it right now.

**Zakhar**

I didn't break the sofa. It broke by itself. Things can't last forever.

(Zakhar, without drying his hands, proceeds to look for the letter, leaving stains all over the place.)

**Oblomov**

Haven't you found it yet?

(Zakhar finds some old letters wedged in behind a book. He brings them to Oblomov.)

**Zakhar**

Here's some kind of letters.

**Oblomov**

No, these are five years old. Now, help me out of the bath.

**Zakhar**

(washing is hands of the whole affair) Well, that's all there are. (he rubs Oblomov down)

**Oblomov**

Get out, I'll find it myself. (Zakhar helps Oblomov on with his robe and, offended, by Oblomov's remark, starts to leave) Where are you going now? (back in bed)

**Zakhar**

What torture. I wish I were dead. What is it now?

**Oblomov**

My handkerchief. Why do you always have to be told?

**Zakhar**

How should I know where your dirty handkerchief is? Maybe it's in your gown someplace. (pointing to the sumptuous folds of Oblomov's gown.)

**Oblomov**

(upset) You always lose everything. This time you're got to look everywhere.

(This Zakhar proceeds to do, pulling out drawers, looking under the bed, etc. Oblomov grows more and more petulant. Finally, Zakhar spots a corner of it under Oblomov.)

**Zakhar**

Ha! (angrily) There it is! Underneath you. You're lying on top of it and you want me to find it. (menacingly) Is this one of your tricks?

(Oblomov, realizing he has been in the wrong, finds something else to blame Zakhar for.)

**Oblomov**

How spotless you keep everything! The dust! The dirt!

**Zakhar**

What dust? What dirt? I sweep almost every day, see—it's clean. (pointing to the chair and table) What more do you want?

**Oblomov**

(pointing to the walls) What about that? (pointing to the ceiling) And that? And (triumphantly) that! (pointing to the remains of a meal, dishes and a bottle on the table)

**Zakhar**

Well, I suppose I could take this away.

**Oblomov**

Is that all? What about the dust on the walls? And the cobwebs?

**Zakhar**

I do all that before Easter.

**Oblomov**

And the books and the pictures?

**Zakhar**

Books and pictures, before Christmas.

**Oblomov**

Don't you know that dust breeds moths? I sometimes even see bedbugs and roaches on the wall.

**Zakhar**

(indifferently) And I've got fleas.

**Oblomov**

Disgusting!

**Zakhar**

Is it my fault there are bugs in the world? Do you think I invented them?

**Oblomov**

It's because of the dirt.

**Zakhar**

Did I invent dirt?

**Oblomov**

And you've got mice in here. I hear them running about at night.

**Zakhar**

I didn't invent mice either—mice—moths—bedbugs—there's plenty of them everywhere—

**Oblomov**

And, why is it other people don't have them, if you please?

**Zakhar**

(with calm conviction) They've got 'em, too.

**Oblomov**

Nonsense.

**Zakhar**

They just hide it from outsiders.

**Oblomov**

You sweep, clean the filth from out of the corners, and there won't be any.

**Zakhar**

You can't go crawling into the cracks after every bug you see.—Besides, clean up dirt today, and it will be back again tomorrow.

**Oblomov**

If it is—sweep it up again.

**Zakhar**

Surely, you're mad. Every day—like a scullery maid. I'd rather be dead.

**Oblomov**

Why are other people's houses clean? Look at those Germans across the street.

**Zakhar**

(with great contempt) And, where would such people get dirt from? The way they live.

**Oblomov**

It's no good talking. You'd better start cleaning up.

**Zakhar**

Many a time I would have done it. It's you who won't let me.

**Oblomov**

There you go again! Blame me.

**Zakhar**

Of course, I blame you. Who else? How am I going to clean this place up with you always lying in bed? Why don't you go out for the afternoon like other people—?

**Oblomov**

What an idea. Why should I have to go out?

**Zakhar**

So I can clean up, of course. But, I'll need some women to help with the scrubbing.

**Oblomov**

What a fantastic idea. Hire some women! (the clock strikes eleven) It's eleven o'clock and I still haven't gotten up and shaved. Zakhar! Zakhar!

**Zakhar**

Now what?

**Oblomov**

Is the water ready for shaving?

**Zakhar**

It's been ready a long time; why don't you get up?

**Oblomov**

(ready with an excuse) Why didn't you tell me? I'd have got up long ago. But first, I've go to write a letter.

**Zakhar**

In that case, you may as well pay these bills.

**Oblomov**

(annoyed) What bills?

**Zakhar**

The butcher, the laundress, the greengrocer—they're all asking for money.

**Oblomov**

(petulantly) Couldn't you give me these bills one at a time, instead of all at once?

**Zakhar**

You—you're the one always says they can wait until tomorrow.

**Oblomov**

Well, and why can't they?

**Zakhar**

No—they're pestering me to death and they won't give me any more credit.

**Oblomov**

Nothing but money and trouble. Well, what are you standing there for? Put them on the table—I'll look at them after I shave.— You say the water is ready?

**Zakhar**

It's ready— Oh, I forgot to tell you—the landlord says we must move.

**Oblomov**

Well, what of it? We'll move— You've already told me about moving three times.

**Zakhar**

That's true. But, we haven't moved, and the landlord says unless we move this time, he'll go to the police.

**Oblomov**

What a bother! We'll move as soon as the weather improves. In a month.

**Zakhar**

He says we must move by Wednesday—

**Oblomov**

What am I to do—? I don't want to hear any more about it. You take care of it.

**Zakhar**

And, what am I to do—?

**Oblomov**

That's your way of getting out of things! Ask me! As if I knew— Do whatever you like, so long as you arrange things so we don't have to move.

**Zakhar**

(in a pitiful state of confusion, whining) I don't see how you can avoid moving out of someone's house if they're putting you out—

**Oblomov**

(indignant) Why are you so helpless?

(There is a knock at the door. Zakhar exits to admit a visitor. Zakhar returns)

**Zakhar**

There's someone to see you.

**Oblomov**

(annoyed) Can't you say I'm not here?

**Zakhar**

I already said you were in.

**Oblomov**

Well, tell him I'm sick or—

**Zakhar**

No.

**Oblomov**

No? Why not?

**Zakhar**

That would be the sin of lying.

**Oblomov**

But how can I see anyone so early in the day?

**Zakhar**

It's almost noon.

**Oblomov**

Besides, I have too many things to do.

**Zakhar**

Eh?

**Oblomov**

I can't have people just swarming around when I'm so busy. It's so much—(distastefully)—work, confusion. Who is it, anyway?

**Zakhar**

Mr. Alekseyev, your old friend from the office—

**Oblomov**

Oh, Alekseyev, hmm. If I didn't have so much to do, I'd really like to see him.

(Enter Alekseyev, a man about Oblomov's age, but otherwise, a rather nondescript individual.)

**Alekseyev**

(extending his hands) How are you, Ilya? I hope I'm not disturbing you?

**Oblomov**

Don't come near! Don't come near! You've just come in from the cold.

**Alekseyev**

Not up yet! Why, it's nearly noon. What's that dressing gown you're wearing?

(Alekseyev looks for a place to put his hat, but each time recoils because of the filth. Eventually, he holds his hat in his hand and ends up twirling it.)

**Oblomov**

It's not a dressing gown, it's a robe. But, why are you out so early?

**Alekseyev**

To see my tailor. How do you like my coat? (pirouetting around)

**Oblomov**

Splendid. But why so wide in the back?

**Alekseyev**

It's a riding coat.

(Zakhar tries to take Alekseyev's hat and reluctantly Alekseyev gives it to him. Zakhar exits.)

**Oblomov**

(aghast) You mean you ride?

**Alekseyev**

Doesn't everyone?

**Oblomov**

Not quite everyone. I never do.

**Alekseyev**

(astounded) Really, why not? Shy of horses?

**Oblomov**

Oh, no. I like horses, but riding is so complicated.

**Alekseyev**

Complicated? Ha, ha. I never heard anyone say that—

**Oblomov**

Yes, you have to mount the horse from one side—I could never remember which it was.

**Alekseyev**

The left. The left.

**Oblomov**

To be sure. But I always forget. Besides, the horse had a tendency to move, and all that bouncing around. No, no, a sled or carriage is as much as I can manage.

**Alekseyev**

But there's nothing like riding, really.

**Oblomov**

Isn't it somewhat fatiguing?

**Alekseyev**

On the contrary, very invigorating. But the reason I came is that Misha Goryunov received his commission.

**Oblomov**

What of it?

**Alekseyev**

Of it? I've come to fetch you.

**Oblomov**

(apprehensively) To go where?

**Alekseyev**

Why, to Misha's.

**Oblomov**

(annoyed) What does he want with me?

**Alekseyev**

Why, he's invited you to dinner, and expressly detailed me to fetch you. And, afterwards to the park.

**Oblomov**

But, what is there to do there?

**Alekseyev**

Why, it's a holiday. There'll be fireworks and a parade. The royal family will be there.

**Oblomov**

Sit down and we'll think about it.

**Alekseyev**

Do get up.

**Oblomov**

Wait a bit. It's early.

**Alekseyev**

Since you won't ride, how shall we go—on foot or by carriage?

**Oblomov**

Well, neither.

**Alekseyev**

But, everyone will be there.

**Oblomov**

Not quite everyone.

**Alekseyev**

My dear, Ilya, the most attractive women will be there.

**Oblomov**

What should I do there?

**Alekseyev**

You could admire the ladies.

**Oblomov**

Me? Admire the ladies!! Ridiculous. But, why have you taken up with Misha Goryunov?

**Alekseyev**

You won't tell?

**Oblomov**

Word of honor.

**Alekseyev**

I'm in love with his sister, Olga.

**Oblomov**

Aha—I knew you had an ulterior motive for hanging around with that bore. So—it's the sister you like?

**Alekseyev**

(forgetting himself and sitting down) Yes, yes, the divine Olga. (remembering himself and jumping up) What a lot of dust. (brushing himself off fussily)

**Oblomov**

That's Zakhar!

**Alekseyev**

How about it?

**Oblomov**

How about what?

**Alekseyev**

Are you going to come?

**Oblomov**

(indolently) Oh, no. I've too much to do.

**Alekseyev**

By the way, have you read my poem?

**Oblomov**

Was it in the papers?

**Alekseyev**

No, in a magazine.

**Oblomov**

Then I haven't read it.

**Alekseyev**

It's entitled "The love of a swindler for a fallen woman."

**Oblomov**

Well, that's certainly an uplifting title. What's it about?

**Alekseyev**

It satirizes our whole society mercilessly— It has the ring of Swift—of Voltaire— A savage satire on vice.

**Oblomov**

How can there be poetry in that? Anyway, I find verse tiresome. Isn't writing poetry a little—difficult?

**Alekseyev**

Well, you've got to apply yourself—

**Oblomov**

When do you find time for it?

**Alekseyev**

Oh, late at night.

**Oblomov**

And you visit many people?

**Alekseyev**

Oh, not more than a dozen a day—

**Oblomov**

Unfortunate man. When do you stop to rest?

**Alekseyev**

Who wants to stop to rest? It's important to be in the swing of things.

**Oblomov**

But don't you find it a bother to go about day after day, ceaselessly?

**Alekseyev**

The things you say! Well, if you won't go, I must—

**Oblomov**

Wait! I want your advice about something.

**Alekseyev**

(glancing at his watch) No time. Another day. Why don't you have lunch with me on Friday? You can tell me about it then.

**Oblomov**

But that would mean I'd have to go out. Wait, please.

**Alekseyev**

All right. I've got a few minutes.

**Oblomov**

Zakhar! Zakhar!

**Zakhar**

(entering) What now?

**Oblomov**

Have you found that letter yet?

**Zakhar**

How am I to find it?

**Oblomov**

Oh, you're so helpless. Do I have to do everything myself?

**Zakhar**

(stomping around looking ineffectively for the letter here and there) When will this torture end?

**Alekseyev**

Ilya, since I'm here, it occurs to me, you know I've been promoted at the office, you know—

**Oblomov**

Yes, I've heard. Head of Department. My, my, congratulations. You deserve it. (Oblomov is never jealous, his congratulations are sincere)

**Alekseyev**

Thank you, Ilya— I knew you'd be pleased. But now, I've got twice as much to do as before.

**Oblomov**

Good Lord. There was plenty enough before.

**Alekseyev**

It's too bad you left.

**Oblomov**

Oh, I couldn't stand getting up practically every day of the week at the crack of dawn. Besides, I have so much work to do on my estate, that it was just too much—

**Alekseyev**

But, many people take care of their estates and hold down civil service jobs—

**Oblomov**

But, to go out in all kinds of weather simply to get to the office when one has enough to live on—it seems so unnecessary.

**Alekseyev**

Hmm. But you really did good work.

**Oblomov**

But, I never could keep up with the pace. There were always so many papers that had to be signed. No matter how much I did, no matter how furiously I drudged signing my name, the in-box always seemed to be full at the end of the day.

**Alekseyev**

(laughing) Sometimes I think you're serious.

**Oblomov**

Come, have dinner with me. We'll drink to your good luck.

**Alekseyev**

Can't. I've got to go to Misha's.

**Oblomov**

Bah Misha! Tell me what's new at the office while Zakhar is finding that letter.

**Alekseyev**

Oh, lots of things. We have to keep records in triplicate now. It's supposed to be a reform. Too much getting lost before.

**Oblomov**

That's true. I was always losing things. What about our former comrades?

**Alekseyev**

Not much. Grushaka is married. Svinkin lost a file of documents, and the Director says he did it on purpose.

**Oblomov**

Impossible. He wouldn't do that.

**Alekseyev**

It will turn up. But the Director is giving me a great deal of grief about it.

**Oblomov**

Well, I can see that you're kept busy. You really work.

**Alekseyev**

Terrible, terrible. But the Director's a very good man.

**Oblomov**

Is your salary good?

**Alekseyev**

Oh, very good. Twelve hundred roubles plus a travel allowance.

**Oblomov**

(getting out of bed) Not bad! Not bad! About as much as an opera star. Still, working from eight to five and then taking work home with you. Not for me.

**Alekseyev**

Actually, Ilya, I need an assistant, and I thought of you—

**Oblomov**

(flattered and horrified) Me? Whatever gave you that idea?

**Alekseyev**

Well, you know the work very well— There'd be no need to train you.

**Oblomov**

Yes, I know the work—(considering)—but—

**Alekseyev**

And, I thought you might prefer coming to work to being shut up here.

**Oblomov**

But, going to work is such a bother. It gets dark before it's time to go home. I hate going home in the dark.

**Alekseyev**

Well, if you like, you can leave early.

**Oblomov**

(protesting) But I'm managing my estate. It's a full time job. I'm working on a new plan—introducing improvements—agonizing work, really.

**Alekseyev**

Even a half day would be good. I could offer you a thousand roubles plus travel—

**Oblomov**

It's very generous, but impossible. This estate is a full time job, I assure you. I can hardly manage it with all the energy I devote to it.

**Alekseyev**

Think it over. You don't have to decide now.

**Oblomov**

I'll certainly think it over. But I'm just not an eight to five person.

**Alekseyev**

Who is? Think it over. I'll drop in again in a few days.

**Oblomov**

Do stay a little longer. I want your advice about this letter I received.

**Alekseyev**

Come on, get dressed. We'll go to Misha's and talk about the letter when we get back. Zakhar will have found the letter by then.

**Oblomov**

It's too early to get dressed.

**Alekseyev**

Early! Why, we're invited for dinner at two. Actually, if we don't hurry, we'll be late.

**Oblomov**

But, I can't dress. Zakhar hasn't pressed up my clothes yet.

**Alekseyev**

Well, tell him to do so. It won't take a minute. I'll just look around while you do. (walking around the room, looking at a picture, then a book, giving a little whistle, mildly disturbed by the dust)

**Oblomov**

(who has not stirred) Whatever are you doing?

**Alekseyev**

(amused) You're back in bed?

**Oblomov**

Is there any reason to get up?

**Alekseyev**

Of course. They're waiting for us. You wanted to go.

**Oblomov**

Go where? I don't want to go somewhere.

**Alekseyev**

See here, Ilya, we just agreed you'd go to Misha's and later to the Park—

**Oblomov**

Me? In this damp weather? I'd probably catch my death.

**Alekseyev**

It's the best weather we've had in months.

**Oblomov**

And, what is there to see? It's overcast.

**Alekseyev**

There's not a cloud in the sky. It only looks overcast because your windows haven't been washed properly.

**Oblomov**

Yes, and if you so much as mention it to Zakhar, he'll insist on hiring women to do it, and forcing me out of the house for a whole day.

**Alekseyev**

Well, what a splendid opportunity to hoist him on his own petard. Just come along to dinner and let him wash the place. He'll have no excuse—

**Oblomov**

(aghast) Leave the house?

**Alekseyev**

That's what one usually does when one goes out for dinner. Don't you want to go?

**Oblomov**

You keep coming back to the same thing! Why can't you stay here? Isn't it nice here?

**Alekseyev**

(guardedly) Oh, very nice, of course. (looking apprehensively for a clean place to sit)

**Oblomov**

Then, spend the day here, and have dinner with me. In the evening you can go to the Park. Oh, I completely forgot. Today is Saturday, and Tarantyev is coming to dine.

**Alekseyev**

Hmm, Tarantyev. (smothering distaste)

**Oblomov**

Now that you've decided to stay, I'll tell you about my affairs.

**Alekseyev**

(surprised) Your affairs?

**Oblomov**

Why do you suppose I am late rising? I've been THINKING!

**Alekseyev**

(even more surprised) Indeed?

**Oblomov**

I don't know what to do.

**Alekseyev**

What on earth has happened?

**Oblomov**

First, I'm being evicted, for no reason.

**Alekseyev**

Have you got a lease?

**Oblomov**

It's expired.

**Alekseyev**

What will you do?

**Oblomov**

Nothing.

**Alekseyev**

Nothing?

**Oblomov**

I don't even want to think about it. Zakhar will simply have to do something.

**Alekseyev**

Some people like to move.

**Oblomov**

Well, let them! I can not endure any sort of change. But, this is a minor problem. Wait till you see this letter, this terrible letter. Now, where can it be? Zakhar! Zakhar!

**Zakhar**

(entering) Oh, Mother of God, when will the Good Lord end my sufferings?

**Oblomov**

Haven't you found the letter?

**Zakhar**

How can I find it? You know I can't read.

**Oblomov**

Look for it anyway.

**Zakhar**

But I haven't seen it since yesterday—

**Oblomov**

Then, where is it? I haven't swallowed it. I remember precisely that you took the letter from me and put it—somewhere. Why can't you ever remember?

**Zakhar**

I think—have you looked under the blankets?

(Zakhar gives the blanket a quick shake.)

**Oblomov**

So, that's where it is? Now, why did you put it there?

**Zakhar**

(finding the letter, outraged) Me! Me?

**Oblomov**

You'd forget your head if I wasn't here to ask you where you'd put it. Now, go make us some tea—

**Zakhar**

(going out) Jesus, Mary, and Joseph and all the Saints—

**Oblomov**

(giving the letter to Alekseyev) Here, read it.

**Alekseyev**

Hmmm—rambles a bit—crop failures—floods— Aha, so that's why he's beating around the bush. Two thousand roubles a year less than last year.

**Oblomov**

I'll die of starvation— What will I do— What will I live on?

**Alekseyev**

Well, it's a great loss. But, perhaps, things will work out? It's only an estimate.

**Oblomov**

Well, if it's only an estimate, why does he have to upset me in advance? Now I'll worry to death.

**Alekseyev**

These peasants have no tact.

**Oblomov**

Well, what would you do in my place?

**Alekseyev**

Perhaps you should go to your estate? Personally take charge—

**Oblomov**

Go to my estate. Personally take charge. What a thought!

**Alekseyev**

Well, it's only a suggestion.

**Oblomov**

Can't you think of something else? My estate is so far away— If only Stolz would come. Stolz always knows what to do.

**Alekseyev**

Stolz—hmmm—

(Suddenly there is a violent knocking at the door. Both jump.)

**Alekseyev**

Speak of the devil, I guess.

**Oblomov**

No, no. Stolz doesn't ring like that. It's Tarantyev.

**Alekseyev**

(trembling) Tarantyev.

(Enter Tarantyev. His booming voice is heard off: "Well, is he home?" He sounds like Zeus the Thunderer himself. Zakhar's voice: "Does he ever go out?" Tarantyev is tall, heavy-set, bearded, coarse, slovenly, and powerful as a bear. He is indifferent to personal grooming and clothes style. He is hostile and cynical. His gestures are bold and sweeping—and he always makes a great commotion, for he loves noise. He is a proletarian and proud of it. When he enters, Alekseyev cringes into a corner and is completely ignored by Tarantyev, who goes directly to Oblomov.)

**Oblomov**

Ah, Tarantyev.

**Tarantyev**

Greetings, friend. And why are you lying in bed at this hour? (approaching the bed and holding out a hairy paw)

**Oblomov**

Don't come near! Don't come near! You've just come in from the cold!

**Tarantyev**

What do you mean cold! Come, take a hand when it's offered to you. (grabbing Oblomov's hand in a crushing grip and pumping it vigorously) Come, now—before I lift you out myself.

**Oblomov**

(hurriedly sitting up and putting his feet in his slippers) I was just getting up.

**Tarantyev**

I know you were getting up: you'd be lying there till dinner time. Hey, Zakhar, you old wretch. Come dress your master, and be quick about it.

**Zakhar**

(entering) Who are you calling a wretch? (with a malevolent stare) You've tracked up the floor with mud like a peddler.

**Tarantyev**

The monster still talks too much. (aiming a lazy but powerful kick at Zakhar)

**Zakhar**

(furious) You just try touching me! I'm going— (Zakhar retreats to the other door)

**Oblomov**

Oh, leave him alone, Tarantyev. Come Zakhar—help me out of bed.

(Zakhar dodges around Tarantyev to reach the bed. Oblomov, leaning on Zakhar like a wounded soldier, moves to the armchair. Zakhar brushes and pomades Oblomov's hair. Meanwhile, Tarantyev has discovered Alekseyev )

**Tarantyev**

(menacingly) Oh, so you're here too— What are you doing here? I've been meaning to tell you what a swine that relative of yours is—

**Alekseyev**

(terrified) What relative? I have no relatives—

**Tarantyev**

Afanasyev, that's who. What do you mean he's not your relative? He's your cousin.

**Alekseyev**

My name is Alekseyev, and he's not my cousin—or my relative—

**Tarantyev**

He must be your relative—he looks like you—exactly. And he's a swine. Tell him that when you see him.

**Alekseyev**

Never laid eyes on him.

**Tarantyev**

Well, I borrowed fifty roubles from him once. Now, that's a small sum. You'd think he'd forget it. But, no. He's been pestering me for almost two years about it. Yesterday, he even followed me to my office. "It's payday," he said. "Now you can repay me." Did I go for him! I disgraced him before everyone; he couldn't find the door quick enough. (solemnly) I've never seen such a swine as that relative of yours. (to Oblomov) Give us a cigar, friend.

**Oblomov**

The cigars are on the table in a box.

**Zakhar**

Will you shave now?

**Oblomov**

I'll wait a bit.

**Tarantyev**

(annoyed) Still the same old ones. I told you to get some Havanas.

**Oblomov**

Still the same.

**Tarantyev**

See that you get some Havanas by next Saturday, or it'll be a long time before you see me again! These are simply vile, you know. (lighting up and puffing) Impossible for a civilized person to smoke them.

**Oblomov**

You've come early today.

**Tarantyev**

What's the matter—getting tired of me?

**Oblomov**

No, no. But you usually come just in time for dinner.

**Tarantyev**

I came early to find out what's for dinner. You always feed me such trash.

**Oblomov**

Ask Zakhar.

**Tarantyev**

Zakhar, what's for dinner?

**Zakhar**

Beef and veal. (ducking out again)

**Tarantyev**

Ah, my dear Ilya, you don't know how to live. And you, a landowner and gentleman. Well, at least you must have some champagne.

**Oblomov**

If not, we can send for some.

**Tarantyev**

Here. Give me the money. I'll pick it up.

**Oblomov**

Champagne costs seven—here's ten.

**Tarantyev**

Let's have it—I'll be back shortly.

**Oblomov**

Wait—I want to ask your advice about something.

**Tarantyev**

What is it? Be quick, I have no time.

**Oblomov**

You see, they are putting me out of my apartment.

**Tarantyev**

You probably don't pay your rent. Serves you right.

**Oblomov**

Nonsense. I always pay in advance. They want the apartment for something else.

**Tarantyev**

Why ask me? Why not ask that thing, or his swinish cousin—?

**Oblomov**

You're a practical man.

**Tarantyev**

(thinking) Very well. I have it. Tomorrow, you must move.

**Oblomov**

What kind of advice is that? I could have told myself that—

**Tarantyev**

(shouting) Don't interrupt. Tomorrow, you must move into my friend's house.

**Oblomov**

Where?

**Tarantyev**

In the Vyborg district.

**Oblomov**

(shuddering) But there are wolves there in the winter!

**Tarantyev**

That needn't concern you. You never go out anyway.

**Oblomov**

But, what if they should come in?

**Tarantyev**

Nonsense. Wolves don't come in.

**Oblomov**

But, nobody lives there.

**Tarantyev**

Nonsense. My friend lives there.

**Oblomov**

It's practically a wilderness.

**Tarantyev**

My friend is a widow with two children. Lives with her brother. He's a sharp one, not like that fellow (pointing to Alekseyev) or his swinish cousin.

**Oblomov**

But, what has it to do with me? I'm not going to move there.

**Tarantyev**

We shall see about that! If you ask my advice, you must take it. I'll move you myself.

**Oblomov**

(with surprising energy) I am not going to move!

**Tarantyev**

To hell with you, then! What's the attraction here?

**Oblomov**

Everything's here. Shops, theatres—my friends. It's right in the center of everything.

**Tarantyev**

And why the devil do you have to be in the center of everything? You never go out.

**Oblomov**

Why, lots of reasons—

**Tarantyev**

For example?

(Oblomov tries to think of some reasons, but cannot, and falls silent.)

**Tarantyev**

(triumphant) You see! Now, in my friend's house everything will be peaceful. No one will ever come to see you except me. (Oblomov winces) And think of all the money you will save. She has been wanting a quiet, reliable tenant for some time. (Oblomov shakes his head) Don't be stupid. You have to move.

It will cost you half what you're spending here. Your food will be twice as good. She's an excellent cook, and Zakhar won't be able to steal the way he has.

**Zakhar**

(overhearing this) Arghh!

**Tarantyev**

There will be more order. This place is never clean—in fact, it's disgusting. There, a women will look after things. You can get rid of Zakhar or send him back to the estate.

**Zakhar**

(with rising indignation) ARGGHHH!

**Oblomov**

(amazed) Rid of Zakhar?

**Tarantyev**

Let the old dog go to pasture.— Why hesitate? Move and be done with it.

**Oblomov**

But, to move into a wilderness, without rhyme or reason. What a wild idea. I don't want to change. If only Stolz were here— He'd find a way—

**Tarantyev**

It's all settled then. You must move. I'll skip dinner and go tell her. She'll be delighted—

**Oblomov**

Wait a minute. Wait a minute. I've got another problem.

**Tarantyev**

Eh? What's that?

**Oblomov**

You've got to read this letter.

**Tarantyev**

Where is it?

**Oblomov**

Where is it? Damn! Zakhar has lost it, again. Zakhar! Zakhar!

**Alekseyev**

(timidly) Here it is—on the blanket—

**Oblomov**

(handing the letter to Tarantyev) Well, what do you think?

**Tarantyev**

You are ruined. Absolutely ruined.

**Oblomov**

What shall I do?

**Tarantyev**

Oh, ask him—or his lout of a cousin.

**Oblomov**

I'm asking you.

**Tarantyev**

All right. Your steward is a thief. Don't believe a word of it.

**Oblomov**

But, it sounds so convincing.

**Tarantyev**

That proves he's a thief. What honest man can write convincingly?

**Oblomov**

But, what shall I do?

**Tarantyev**

Replace him at once.

**Oblomov**

With whom? I haven't been there in twelve years.

**Tarantyev**

Go there at once. Raise hell. Take charge.

**Oblomov**

That's what Alekseyev said.

**Tarantyev**

Did he, the swine? If you don't go, you're done for. That thief will make off with everything.

**Oblomov**

(suddenly) You go. You.

**Tarantyev**

What am I, your manager?

**Oblomov**

Then, what am I to do?

**Tarantyev**

Ask your neighbors, perhaps?

**Oblomov**

I shall write them the day after tomorrow.

**Tarantyev**

Sit down and write at once.

**Oblomov**

But, the mail doesn't leave till the day after tomorrow. I can write tomorrow.

**Tarantyev**

You're a lost man.

**Oblomov**

What more do you want?

**Tarantyev**

Sit down and write.

**Oblomov**

Couldn't you do it?

**Tarantyev**

Me? Oh, you sluggard.

**Oblomov**

If only Stolz were here. He'd fix everything.

**Tarantyev**

That damned German!

**Oblomov**

See here, Tarantyev, please be more careful about what you say, especially about someone close to me.

**Tarantyev**

Close to you!

**Oblomov**

He's closer to me than any relative. We were raised together. I will not permit you—

**Tarantyev**

Ah, if you prefer a German to me, I will never set foot in your house again—

**Oblomov**

You ought to respect him as MY friend—

**Tarantyev**

Respect a German? For what?

**Oblomov**

I've already told you: because I grew up with him, and went to school with him.

**Tarantyev**

Who cares? You went to school with lots of people. You might even have gone to school with his cousin. (pointing to Alekseyev) Am I supposed to respect that swine because you went to school with him?

**Oblomov**

If he were here, he would solve everything, without insisting on champagne and Havana cigars.

**Tarantyev**

Oh! Now, you reproach me! To hell with you and your champagne. (he spits out the cigar and crushes it underfoot) Here, take your money. Now, where have I put it? I can't remember what I did with those damned roubles. (pulling out a greasy piece of paper) No, that's not it. Now, where did I put it?

**Oblomov**

Don't trouble yourself. I'm not reproaching you. I only want you to speak decently of a man who has done so much for me.

**Tarantyev**

He's going to do much more for you. Just wait.

**Oblomov**

What do you mean?

**Tarantyev**

When your German friend fleeces you, you'll know what it is to prefer a Russian to (pronouncing the word with unspeakable contempt) a GERMAN.

**Oblomov**

Listen, Tarantyev!

**Tarantyev**

No more listening. I've had enough of you. God knows how many insults I've endured. My father warned me to beware of Germans. Look at his father, for example.

**Oblomov**

What's wrong with Stolz's father?

**Tarantyev**

Look at all the money he made.

**Oblomov**

He did it honestly—

**Tarantyev**

Honestly! Do you think a Russian, a good Russian, would do all that— No, no— There's something shady about him.

**Oblomov**

But, he invested, and saved—

**Tarantyev**

Bah! And the son—he's always got his nose in a book. Probably figuring some swindle—

**Oblomov**

Let's drop it— Go get the champagne, and I'll write the letters.

**Tarantyev**

All right. Oh, I forgot. I want to borrow your dress coat tomorrow. I'm going to a wedding.

**Oblomov**

It won't fit—

**Tarantyev**

Of course it will. It will look as though it were made for me. Besides, you never wear it. Zakhar! Zakhar!!

**Zakhar**

(entering) Arghh! (but he won't fully enter the room)

**Tarantyev**

Come here, you old brute. (Zakhar won't come any further) Call him, Ilya. What's the matter with him, I wonder?

**Oblomov**

Zakhar.

**Zakhar**

(responding to his master) Damnation! (he finally enters with a terrible thud)

**Oblomov**

Bring my dress coat. Tarantyev wants to see if it fits him.

**Zakhar**

(defiantly) I will not give it to him!

**Tarantyev**

Why don't you send him to a house of correction, Ilya?

**Oblomov**

We won't come to that. Bring the coat, Zakhar: don't be obstinate.

**Zakhar**

No, let him first bring back the shirt he borrowed six months ago. I'm not going to give him the coat.

**Tarantyev**

Oh, go to the devil! I'll bring back the shirt with the champagne. And, I'm going to rent that apartment for you, Ilya. Do you hear?

**Oblomov**

Very well, very well.

**Tarantyev**

And, see the soup is ready at five— As for you— (grabbing Alekseyev by the sleeve) You come along. I want to talk to you about that swine, your cousin.

**Alekseyev**

He's not my cousin.

**Tarantyev**

A likely story. He looks just like you. Now hop— (he exits nosily, propelling Alekseyev)

**Zakhar**

Arghh.

(Oblomov has returned to the bed; Zakhar, who has been watching Tarantyev has not noticed.)

**Zakhar**

(astonished) Why are you lying down again?

**Oblomov**

Don't bother me. I'm reading.

**Zakhar**

But, the shaving water will be cold?

**Oblomov**

You're right. But first, I want to think.

(Zakhar goes out grumpily; Oblomov passes into a brief reverie, then wakes with a start.)

**Oblomov**

Zakhar! Zakhar!

**Zakhar**

(entering) Now what? I wonder my legs can drag me.

**Oblomov**

Zakhar! I'll tell you what—it's a long time till dinner. I'll have a bit of lunch. There was some cheese left last night.

**Zakhar**

Left!— Where? There wasn't anything left.

**Oblomov**

Of course there was. I remember it quite well.

**Zakhar**

(stubbornly) There wasn't anything left.

**Oblomov**

There was, I tell you.

**Zakhar**

(with finality) There was no such cheese.

**Oblomov**

(reproachfully) You ate it.

**Zakhar**

Me? You accuse me?

**Oblomov**

(with conviction) You ate it.

**Zakhar**

(obstinately) How could I eat it? There was no cheese left.

**Oblomov**

(wearily) Buy some then.

**Zakhar**

Give me money.

**Oblomov**

There's change on the table.

**Zakhar**

(going to the table) Not enough.

**Oblomov**

There were some coppers, too.

**Zakhar**

I don't see any—

**Oblomov**

There were. I took them from a peddler myself.

**Zakhar**

There were no coppers.

**Oblomov**

(with crushing reproach) Zakhar, you took them—

**Zakhar**

(withered but obstinate) There were no coppers.

**Oblomov**

(finding some money) Never mind. Here—and hurry—

(Zakhar goes out muttering "There were no coppers".)

**Oblomov**

What a headache. I really must take everything in hand. Tarantyev is perfectly right. I shall write immediately. I must do something immediately. Immediately. (yawning) Still, there's plenty of time. After a brief nap.

(The lights dim, indicating a short lapse of time. Then, there is a commotion as Zakhar enters clumsily carrying a tray. Zakhar pushes through the door on the left with a tray, managing to bump into everything and knocking off the top of the decanter which rolls noisily on the floor.)

**Oblomov**

(waking up) See what happens! You might at least pick it up.

**Zakhar**

(without putting the tray down, tries to pick up the decanter, but cannot) Arghh.

**Oblomov**

(laughing) Go on, pick it up! What's stopping you?

**Zakhar**

Damnation. (to the decanter) I wish you were at the bottom of the sea. (straightening up) Whoever heard of having lunch right before dinner? (putting the dray down, he picks up the decanter)

(Oblomov begins to eat.)

**Zakhar**

The landlord just sent another message.

(Oblomov says nothing, but continues to eat.)

**Zakhar**

We have to move Wednesday. (pause) What are you going to do?

**Oblomov**

(rising) What a venomous man you are, Zakhar. You won't even let me eat. You know I have forbidden you to mention it.

(advancing on Zakhar who backs away, knocking over furniture in his retreat)

**Zakhar**

Why am I venomous? I haven't killed anybody.

**Oblomov**

(advancing) You are poisoning my life.

**Zakhar**

(retreating) I am not venomous.

**Oblomov**

Why do you keep pestering me about the apartment? (advancing)

**Zakhar**

(retreating) Something must be done.

**Oblomov**

What can I do? (advancing)

**Zakhar**

(retreating) What can I do? (bumping) You can write a letter—you might do it—(dares to say it) NOW.

**Oblomov**

(thunderstruck) Now? As if I didn't have more important things to do. (goes back to the desk) No ink! How am I to write?

**Zakhar**

Well, I'll get some more.

**Oblomov**

No paper either. How is it there's no paper in the house? And, you say you're not venomous!

(Zakhar shuffles about and pulls out an ordinary writing sheet.)

**Oblomov**

Do you think I can write a letter on that?

**Zakhar**

Why not?

(Zakhar goes out and returns with ink. Oblomov has almost fallen asleep.)

**Oblomov**

(yawning) Next time, look sharp, Zakhar, and do your work properly. Maybe I can make a draft. (he sits down and dips his pen) "Dear sir—" (writing) What vile ink— (he writes with growing irritation) Oh, damn this letter anyhow! I can't go on racking my brain over such trifles— Here— (tearing the letter into pieces and throwing it on the floor)

**Oblomov**

Zakhar! Do you see all that? (pointing to the mess he has just made)

**Zakhar**

I see it. (pulling bills out of his pockets)

**Oblomov**

Don't pester me anymore about the apartment!

**Zakhar**

All right.

**Oblomov**

Now, what have you got there?

**Zakhar**

Bills.

**Oblomov**

Oh, for Heaven's sake— That again! Will you please pick that stuff up? I have to tell you everything.

(Zakhar picks up the remains of the letter, but nearly knocks over the table in doing so. The ink spills on Oblomov.)

**Oblomov**

Now, see what you've done.

**Zakhar**

(drying him off with a handkerchief) Here.

**Oblomov**

How much do these bills come to—? Be quick.

**Zakhar**

The butcher—eighty roubles—

**Oblomov**

Are you out of your mind? All that for the butcher alone?

**Zakhar**

You haven't paid him for three months.

**Oblomov**

And you say you're not a venomous man. Spending a fortune on meat.

**Zakhar**

It wasn't me that ate it.

**Oblomov**

It wasn't. It wasn't. I suppose it wasn't you that ate the cheese!

**Zakhar**

(savagely) There was no cheese!

**Oblomov**

All right, all right.

**Zakhar**

If you didn't let Tarantyev come here, you'd spend less.

**Oblomov**

But, how do I get you to eat less?

**Zakhar**

Are you at it again?— Reproaching me for eating.

**Oblomov**

What a heap of money! I told you to pay a little at a time. Suddenly, the whole thing has to be paid.

**Zakhar**

Give me the money.

**Oblomov**

Here— Now leave me alone. I have work to do. (returning to bed) What people!

**Zakhar**

Ilya—

**Oblomov**

Are you still here?

**Zakhar**

What am I to tell the landlord?

**Oblomov**

About what?

**Zakhar**

About moving.

**Oblomov**

Are you at it again? You mean to be the death of me. Don't you? Admit it.

**Zakhar**

God be with you. Who wishes you ill?

**Oblomov**

You do! I forbade you to mention moving— You know it upsets me. Do you know what it means to move?

**Zakhar**

Well, it's like going out! You could walk about the street. It's not healthy staying home.

**Oblomov**

Walk about the streets! Stop chattering nonsense. Moving— means noise —breakage—work— That's what moving means: Work! And nowhere to rest—to lie down. It would make me miserable! Do you see what you're exposing me to with your laziness?

**Zakhar**

My laziness!

**Oblomov**

You haven't—you won't—figure out a way to prevent this disaster.

**Zakhar**

But other people move.

**Oblomov**

So, it comes to that! I am no different from other people in your eyes.

**Zakhar**

Pardon me. You know you're very—special—to me.

**Oblomov**

Come here. (Zakhar hesitates) Come here. (Zakhar still hesitates) Here! (Zakhar edges slowly towards him) Nearer!

**Zakhar**

I wish I were dead. (Oblomov stares at him) What is it, sir?

**Oblomov**

Are you sorry for your misbehavior? Your misdemeanor?

**Zakhar**

What's a misdemeanor?

**Oblomov**

Do you understand what you have done? Answer me.

**Zakhar**

Couldn't I just hang myself?

**Oblomov**

Now, aren't you a venomous man? (solemnly) You have grieved me.

**Zakhar**

(almost in tears) How have I grieved you?

**Oblomov**

You think I am like other people. And, what are other people? People who clean their own boots, dress themselves, and pretend to be gentlemen.

**Zakhar**

Germans are like that.

**Oblomov**

But, how can you think I am like that?

**Zakhar**

(gasping) You're very different.

**Oblomov**

Exactly. Have you considered how these other people live? Why, they work without ceasing and—and they even run their own errands. How could you—you who have cared for me since I was a child—have the audacity to compare me to others?

**Zakhar**

(broken) I am sorry.

**Oblomov**

Here I am, beset with cares—working till my head spins—Ingrate—

**Zakhar**

Please don't.

**Oblomov**

Ingrate. I've let you care for me all my life and this is what I get.

**Zakhar**

(strangled) Please, sir.

**Oblomov**

Now I see what a serpent I've been harboring in my bosom.

**Zakhar**

Serpent! (wailing) When have I ever mentioned such vile things?

**Oblomov**

I'm absolutely exhausted. You see what you've done to me?— I'll have to lie down. To atone for your guilt, you have better make some arrangements with the landlord— (yawns, drops off for a minute)

**Zakhar**

But, it will soon be dinner time— Get up! It's disgraceful.

**Oblomov**

You'd better repent.

**Zakhar**

(roaring) Get up, I tell you!

**Oblomov**

(menacingly) What! What!

**Zakhar**

(softly) I said, why don't you get up, sir?

**Oblomov**

How dare you speak so rudely?

**Zakhar**

Rudely! You must have been dreaming.

**Oblomov**

You think I'm sleeping. Well, I'm not. (drowses off)

**Zakhar**

(shouts) Fire! Help! Fire!

**Oblomov**

(jumps up, looks around) Will you stop it? You just wait till I wake up— (about to lie down)

(Stolz enters quietly; he has been watching for about a minute. Stolz roars with laughter.)

**Stolz**

Fire Department, at your service.

**Oblomov**

Stolz! Stolz!

(Oblomov jumps up and embraces Stolz as the curtain falls.)

**CURTAIN**

# ACT II
## SCENE 2: St. Petersburg, a Few Days Later

*The same as Act I. A few days later. The room is noticeably cleaner, the bed is made. Zakhar enters from the kitchen, grumbling.*

**Zakhar** (furious) Cook says I must sweep. I've already swept today. What is there to sweep? (increasingly upset) Who asked her advice? She was hired to cook. Whoever heard of dusting the furniture first, then sweeping? The little chit. The little miss know-it-all. I've been sweeping first, then dusting for fifty years. I'm not going to sweep ten times a day. (he throws the broom down) Women think they know everything about housekeeping—just because they're women. (yelling towards the kitchen) Go back to where you belong. Master hired you to cook. Leave cleaning to me, the expert. Know your place, woman. (stomping around) I don't see why the master hired you in the first place. This is all Stolz's doing. I've cooked for twenty years—no complaints. First thing she did when she got here, she upset everything in the kitchen. I purposely put everything together so I could get at it. And she put it, God knows where. Why? (defiantly) So that the tea and sugar don't taste of soap, she says! Bah! Now, where am I going to find anything? God, what a mess a single woman can make! And not only that, I don't like your cooking! Do you hear? I don't like your cooking, even if master does! (Zakhar goes back out into the kitchen, still grumbling)

(Stolz and Oblomov enter from the street entrance. Oblomov is fashionably dressed and proves a fine looking gentleman.)

**Oblomov**

I haven't had my boots off for days. My feet are killing me. (starting to call Zakhar, but Stolz frowns) Can't I call him this once?

**Stolz**

Remember our bargain. If you could do it for yourself, you do it for yourself.

**Oblomov**

Still—it's hard getting them off.

**Stolz** (sternly) Try.

**Oblomov**

(struggles with his boots) There and (grunt) there. Can I?

**Stolz**

Yes.

**Oblomov**

Zakhar! (Zakhar enters) Put my boots away and bring my slippers.

(Zakhar collects the boots and returns with the slippers, muttering "I don't believe it; it won't last.")

**Oblomov**

I don't like this Petersburg life.

**Stolz**

What sort of life do you like?

**Oblomov**

Well, not this one.

**Stolz**

What exactly don't you like about it?

**Oblomov**

Everything! This eternal competition—gossip— And then, rushing about like flies—it's—fatiguing—. I don't see how I'm more guilty of wasting my life than they are. At least I don't bother anyone dozing at home. What sort of life is that—running about, getting drunk, spreading malicious stories, ogling women? Far better to stay in bed.

**Stolz**

Everyone else is chasing the brass ring. You alone want nothing.

**Oblomov**

And worst of all, for all their frenetic activity, not one of them looks happy.

**Stolz**

And, what is your idea, then?

**Oblomov**

Well, I should move to the country—

**Stolz**

But, you won't even move from this apartment!

**Oblomov**

But staying here is only temporary—

**Stolz**

You've been here ten years.

**Oblomov**

But—in fact—I'm planning to move—into more permanent quarters—

**Stolz**

That's the first I've heard of that—

**Oblomov**

Oh, I've been planning to move practically since I got here. This place really isn't suitable.

**Stolz**

(looking at Oblomov with amazement) Then, why did you make such a fuss about moving?

**Oblomov**

Well, one can't move just like that. I wouldn't have time to find anything—suitable. Anyway, it was kind of you to manage things with the landlord. I can't imagine how you did it.

**Stolz**

Simple. I bribed him. I offered to increase your rent.

**Oblomov**

(aghast) But, why didn't you tell me? How much?

**Stolz**

About fifty roubles a month. You can well afford it. Especially with the additional money your steward is sending.

**Oblomov**

I still can't understand how you did that.

**Stolz**

Nothing could be simpler. I wrote him that unless he rendered up an additional four thousand roubles, you would sack him and prosecute him for embezzlement. Amazing the effect of such a letter on his managerial abilities. And, it probably represents only part of the interest on what he's stolen. He can well afford it. You really ought to sack him.

**Oblomov**

But he's been steward since my father's time. I really can't do that. (Stolz shakes his head) I can't tell you how happy you've made me. I wish I knew how to repay you.

**Stolz**

Keep your promise—break out of this sloth.

**Oblomov**

Well, you see, I'm trying. But it's not easy to do—all at once.

**Stolz**

You were telling me your idea of the good life—tell me more.

**Oblomov**

Well, I should move to the country. In the mornings, I would get up and walk around the estate. Then, I would breakfast with my wife. In the afternoon, bathe or swim. Play with the children. Take another walk before dinner. Listen to music, perhaps. Have you to tea.

**Stolz**

And then?

**Oblomov**

And then, go to bed.

**Stolz**

Every day—just like that?

**Oblomov**

Certainly. What more is there?

**Stolz**

Just sit about with empty hands?

**Oblomov**

(puzzled) What would be in one's hands? A handkerchief, perhaps? Isn't that life?

**Stolz**

No, that is not life.

**Oblomov**

(still perplexed) What is it, then?

**Stolz**

It's—it's Oblomovism!

**Oblomov**

But, good Heavens—what do people work for, if not to be able to retire at ease? Why all this rushing about except to get enough so one can laze about?

**Stolz**

I work.

**Oblomov**

Someday you'll stop.

**Stolz**

(puzzled in his turn) Never. Why should I?

**Oblomov**

When you've reached your goal—doubled your capital—

**Stolz**

I've done that several times already— I shall never stop.

**Oblomov**

Why work hard all your life?

**Stolz**

For the sake of work. Work is the very essence of life. Take away my work and where is my life?

**Oblomov**

How horrible? To live for nothing but work. Surely, that is a disease worse than mine?

**Stolz**

(uncomfortable) Of course, one must stop to smell the flowers. (deliberately changing the subject) As for flowers, I thought it not amiss that you find a little rose to cheer you up and rouse you from this lethargy.

**Oblomov**

A rose? What do you mean? Roses don't do that.

**Stolz**

I mean a woman: Olga Sergeyevna.

**Oblomov**

Oh, yes. You introduced me to her yesterday.

**Stolz**

That's the one.

**Oblomov**

(troubled) But, so vivacious. So overpowering— (frightened) What do you mean, you arranged—I will not pay visits to ladies—

**Stolz**

(easily) That won't be necessary. You can't confine yourself to male society.

**Oblomov**

(uneasily) Just what do you mean?

**Stolz**

Don't you like her?

**Oblomov**

Yes, of course, but—

**Stolz**

Well then, it's all arranged.

**Oblomov**

But I won't go calling on her. Don't think I will go calling— I refuse to go calling on anyone.

**Stolz**

I said, it won't be necessary—

**Oblomov**

(relieved) Good.

**Stolz**

I've arranged for her to call on you.

**Oblomov**

(jumping up) What?

**Stolz**

She's very advanced, radical intelligentsia. But quite respectable.

**Oblomov**

But, but, but—she can't come here—

**Stolz**

Why not?

**Oblomov**

It's unheard of. Besides, she looked at me so intently; it was most—disconcerting. She was positively staring at me as if she wanted to eat me. And, the woman is so energetic— (gestures) All motion—like a whirlwind—

**Stolz**

Yes, she would like to gobble you up. You're quite a catch, you know—good looking—well off—

**Oblomov**

Me—good looking?

**Stolz**

Indeed! The ladies can't believe you've been hiding away so long.

**Oblomov**

(humbly) What an idea! What woman would be interested in me?

**Stolz**

Oh, you've already turned several heads.

**Oblomov**

This is some kind of joke.

**Stolz**

I assure you, it is not. Anastasia Fillipovna and Natalia Ivanovna both told me in unmistakable terms that you would be a most welcome caller. Unfortunately, I had to tell them that there are limits, even to my powers over you.

**Oblomov**

Thank God for limits—

**Stolz**

Olga, however, is made of tougher stuff. "If Mohammed will not go to the mountain, the mountain must go to Mohammed." Her exact words. Fact.

**Oblomov**

What an Amazon! And the way she looks at people. It's agony, I tell you. She looks right into your soul. It's terrifying. You must go to her and stop this. Tell her not to come.

**Stolz**

Nonsense.

(A noise at the door.)

**Oblomov**

Tell her I'm ill. Tell her I've gone to the country, tell her—

**Stolz**

Too late, old friend. She's at the door now.

**Oblomov**

(turning, looking for a place to hide) But, I'm not dressed. The place is filthy. See all that dust. Zakhar! Stolz! Help—

**Stolz**

Buck up, old man. Now or never.

(Enter Olga Sergeyevna. She is beautiful and perfectly in command of every social situation. Although young and unmarried, she has the assurance of a widow. She is emancipated, but has not ceased to be a woman. Rather, she sees her freedom as an enhanced way of expressing her femininity. Oblomov is awestruck by her presence.)

**Olga**

Monsieur Oblomov, I hope you will receive a visitor?

(Oblomov is awestruck, speechless, but still manages to execute a bow which is the more charming because of it's confusion.)

**SHORT CURTAIN**

# ACT II
## SCENE 3: ST. PETERSBURG, A FEW DAYS LATER

*Stolz, Oblomov, and Olga enter from the street door. Stolz is humming an aria: La Donna e mobile.*

**Stolz**

I don't know the reason, Olga, but you sang tonight as you never sang before.

**Olga**

You're too kind.

**Oblomov**

You were magnificent.

**Olga**

(looking fondly at him) Monsieur Oblomov, *tu est tres gallant*.

**Oblomov**

Your singing comes from the heart.

**Olga**

Yes. (pressing her ample bosom) It comes from here. (smiling at him again)

**Oblomov**

(whispering to Stolz) She's looking at me again.

**Stolz**

You're in luck, Ilya.

**Oblomov**

You didn't tell her my socks don't match, did you?

(Olga seats herself on the couch and looks at an album.)

**Olga**

Was this you as a baby?

**Oblomov**

What? I'm sorry.

**Olga**

Was it you?

**Oblomov**

Oh, yes—when I was a child.

**Stolz**

(rising) I have some work to do, Ilya. I must be going. (to Olga) You see, I keep my promises.

**Oblomov**

(low to Stolz) Don't leave. Whatever shall I do? I've never been alone with—

**Stolz**

You're doing fine. She likes you. Be yourself. (loud) This work really won't wait.

**Oblomov**

But, I shall be here all alone—with her!

**Olga**

I'll keep you company.

**Oblomov**

(to Stolz) This is treachery. (to Olga) You are very kind.

**Stolz**

(bowing to Olga who gives him her hand) I'm off— (low) Don't eat him all in one bite.

**Olga**

You leave him in good hands.

**Stolz**

(aside) Experienced hands.

(Stolz exits to the street. A long silence. Olga smiles at Oblomov; Oblomov cringes, but smiles in return—shyly. Oblomov, with a wretched effort, tries to say something, but manages only a crooked grimace.)

**Oblomov**

(in a heroic effort to make conversation) Do—you—like—the theatre?

**Olga**

Not particularly.

**Oblomov**

(in an agony) The ballet, perhaps?

**Olga**

Not at all.

**Oblomov**

(desperate, pathetic) What do you like, then?

**Olga**

(mischievously) Men!

**Oblomov**

(strangled) Ah—

**Olga**

(rising and sitting beside Oblomov) Is it true you find life very dull?

**Oblomov**

Yes. Not really.

**Olga**

(amused by his confusion) Stolz says you are going abroad with him.

**Oblomov**

Yes. Certainly, certainly.

**Olga**

Do you want to go?

**Oblomov**

Certainly. Of course not.

**Olga**

Stolz says it's hard to get you to do anything—

**Oblomov**

I'm a little lazy.

**Olga**

(edging closer) Lazy! Is it possible? I don't understand that in a man.

**Oblomov**

What is there to understand? I just sit at home most of the time.

**Olga**

Where do you sit? Here?

**Oblomov**

Actually—I err—lie in the bed.

(They both look at the bed, Oblomov apprehensively, Olga with anticipation.)

**Olga**

You must read a lot there—

**Oblomov**

(unable to stand the heat, he gets out of the kitchen and stands up) Well, in actuality—I— It's so very hot in here, don't you think?

**Olga**

Hot? It's probably going to get hotter.

**Oblomov**

Do you think so? (mopping his brow) Zakhar! Zakhar!

**Zakhar**

(stomping in) Well, what is it?

**Oblomov**

Can't you open the windows?

**Zakhar**

Are you insane? It's freezing out there. Besides, they're nailed shut.

**Oblomov**

(babbling) Try anyway.

**Zakhar**

(grumbling, goes to the window and rattles it) Hopeless. (he goes out before Oblomov can stop him)

**Olga**

(ironically) Don't feel it your duty as host to entertain me! I'm actually having lots of fun. (she rises) May I walk around?

**Oblomov**

(who has surrendered to his fate) Of course.

(Olga proceeds to look at everything, but winds up very close to Oblomov who retreats. Finally, she maneuvers him into a corner.)

**Olga**

Do you have any secrets?

**Oblomov**

Heavens no! What kind of secrets would I have?

**Olga**

Oh—that you wear unmatched stockings, for example.

**Oblomov**

(hotly) Stolz told you that!

**Olga**

Don't be angry with him. He loves you—really he does. (she puts her hand on the bookcase) My, what dust.

**Oblomov**

It's because of Zakhar! Zakhar! Zakhar!

**Zakhar**

(stomping in) What now?

**Oblomov**

Do you see that, Zakhar?

**Zakhar**

To be sure, I see it.

**Oblomov**

What is it?

**Zakhar**

It's a bookcase, as far as I can tell.

**Oblomov**

It's a dirty bookcase. Dust it.

**Zakhar**

But I can't dust.

**Oblomov**

Why not, if you please?

**Zakhar**

Because Anissya dusts.

**Oblomov**

But, why didn't she dust?

**Zakhar**

She had the morning off.

**Oblomov**

Dust it, then.

**Zakhar**

Can't.

**Oblomov**

Why not?

**Zakhar**

Can't dust when you have company. (he goes out quickly)

**Oblomov**

All right, all right. First thing in the morning, then. Zakhar! Zakhar!

**Zakhar**

(offstage) Well?

**Oblomov**

(helplessly) Err—nothing. Make sure you dust in the morning. Well, that takes care of him.

**Olga**

(agreeing) That takes care of him.

**Oblomov**

I must be boring you.

**Olga**

No—no. You are quite interesting—as a specimen.

**Oblomov**

I seldom have an opportunity to go into society, and I don't make interesting conversation—

**Olga**

You're very entertaining, just being yourself.

**Oblomov**

You're very kind.

**Olga**

(aside) I shall be kinder still. (aloud) You're very—sweet.

**Oblomov**

You're so—polite.

**Olga**

You're very cute.

**Oblomov**

You're so beautiful—

**Olga**

You manage well for someone who has never been in society. (pause) Do you like the company of women, Monsieur Oblomov?

**Oblomov**

Oh, yes—theoretically—

**Olga**

Theoretically?

**Oblomov**

I seldom have the opportunity—

**Olga**

If you were to have an opportunity—?

**Oblomov**

An opportunity—I rarely—

**Olga**

Would you know how to make use of it?

**Oblomov**

I—I—don't know—err—

**Olga**

Have you ever been in love?

**Oblomov**

In love? Me?

**Olga**

Have you ever done anything WICKED with a woman?

**Oblomov**

How should I do that? No, no—you see—I—

**Olga**

I like you better and better—

**Oblomov**

I must be tiring you—

**Olga**

Not at all—I find you very—refreshing—(Oblomov shifts nervously from one foot to the other) You must think of me as your friend. We understand each other so perfectly.

**Oblomov**

We do? (Olga takes his hand)

**Olga**

Of course, Can't you feel it? (pressing his hand to her bosom) I feel it here.

**Oblomov**

(spluttering, trying to disengage his hand) I—I—that is to say—

**Olga**

Don't you feel something EXALTING? (still pressing his hand)

**Oblomov**

Oh yes. I've never been so exalted in my life.

**Olga**

When something like this happens, one must surrender to it.— It happens only once in a lifetime. Don't fight it.

**Oblomov**

Fighting is—fatiguing.

**Olga**

Doubtless you have a sublime will, above mundane, physical matters. You dream great dreams, Monsieur Oblomov. (still pressing his hand)

**Oblomov**

(yawning) I can't recall any. I usually think about dinner, or when I was a child.

**Olga**

I know what you are made of. (she still has his hand)

**Oblomov**

(tugging weakly) Do you?

**Olga**

It's so grand that it puts me all in a tremble. (Olga trembles, every inch of her)

**Oblomov**

How it must tire you.

**Olga**

It makes me feel faint— Ohh! (collapsing into his arms)

**Oblomov**

Olga Sergeyvna!

**Olga**

I'll be all right. Help me to lie down—there. (pointing to the bed)

**Oblomov**

(assisting her to the bed) I will call Zakhar. (Olga hangs about his neck) Zakh— (but she smothers his call with a kiss, he tries again, this time a call for help) ZA! (smothered again)

# BLACKOUT

# ACT II
## SCENE 4: ST. PETERSBURG, THE MORNING OF THE NEXT DAY

*There is a stirring, yawning, in Oblomov's bed. Olga in Oblomov's Persian robe, yawns and sits up.*

**Olga**

Zakhar! Zakhar!

**Oblomov**

(next to her, naked at least to the waist jumps up) What are you doing?

**Olga**

I'm calling Zakhar! I want some breakfast.

**Oblomov**

You can't do that!

**Olga**

Why not, for Heaven's sake? I'm hungry. Famished.

**Oblomov**

But, it's not proper.

**Olga**

I'm dressed, silly. The old goat won't see anything of—me. (pointing to her robe)

(Oblomov suddenly looks at himself, his nakedness and rushes about to put something on, while trying to cover himself from view. Finally, he finds his coat and puts it on, without any shirt. He buttons it up tight.)

**Oblomov**

I wonder where my shirt went? (starting to call) Zak— (but he realizes his mistake and shuts off in mid call; he almost chokes)

(Olga is thoroughly enjoying Oblomov's embarrassment. There is a loud thumping noise off.)

**Oblomov**

(frantic) That's Zakhar! Under the blankets, quick! He mustn't see you here.

**Olga**

(protesting) This is ridiculous!

**Oblomov**

(pushing her under the blankets) Quick!

(Zakhar enters with a broom, bucket, mop, pail, and feather

duster. He clanks along clumsily, catching the mop in the door.)

**Zakhar**

I thought I heard you calling, sir.

**Oblomov**

Me! Calling? Ridiculous!

**Zakhar**

Yes, you.

**Oblomov**

You must be hearing things.

**Zakhar**

Strange, I could have sworn—

(Olga peeps out from under the covers; Zakhar does not see her, but Oblomov does and pushes her back.)

**Zakhar**

Well, I'm here anyway. I'm going to give this place a thorough cleaning. A little dust upsets you so.

**Oblomov**

Dust, upset me? What are you talking about?

**Zakhar**

I'm going to clean this place once and for all. I'm tired of your endless complaints.

**Oblomov**

Who's complaining? Me, complain about dust!

**Zakhar**

You are—who else? Never give me any peace about it. Well, when I'm finished, you won't be able to find any dust with a microscope. Now, clear out so I can make the bed and get to work.

**Oblomov**

(in great agitation) It really isn't necessary at this time.

**Zakhar**

(astounded) Eh?

**Oblomov**

Do it later.

**Zakhar**

Didn't you tell me last night to do it this morning?

**Oblomov**

Last night?

**Zakhar**

Last night!

**Oblomov**

I don't seem to remember.

**Zakhar**

Well, I do. Now, if you'll just clear out, I'll start with the bed— (moving toward the bed)

**Oblomov**

(horrified and putting himself between Zakhar and the bed) You mustn't do that.

**Zakhar**

Why not? You're up and dressed.

**Oblomov**

You can't start there!

**Zakhar**

Yes, I can. You'll see.

(The blankets heave up and down with Olga's suppressed laughter.)

**Oblomov**

(blocking Zakhar who has again started toward the bed) You'd better do it some other time.

**Zakhar**

But, Anissya says you must make the bed first, then dust. Just let me make it. It will only take a minute.

**Oblomov**

(blocking him) No. No.

**Zakhar**

(puzzled) But, why not?

**Oblomov**

I may want to lie down again.

**Zakhar**

Well, then lie down—who's stopping you? I'll make it again.

**Oblomov**

(another block) No. No.

**Zakhar**

But, why not?

**Oblomov**

Why not?

**Zakhar**

Why not?

**Oblomov**

Because there's no need.

**Zakhar**

But the bed is unmade.

**Oblomov**

True.

**Zakhar**

Therefore, it needs to be made.

**Oblomov**

Nonsense.

**Zakhar**

Anyway, you're dressed.

**Oblomov**

So I am.

**Zakhar**

But, where's your shirt?

**Oblomov**

My shirt?

**Zakhar**

Your shirt.

**Oblomov**

(lapsing) I don't know. Where did you put it?

**Zakhar**

Me? YOU probably left it in the bed! (lurching towards the bed)

**Oblomov**

(blocking again) That's all right, that's all right.

**Zakhar**

You're always blaming me, when you do it yourself. It's probably right under the blanket.

**Oblomov**

I'll find it myself.

**Zakhar**

(thunderstruck) Eh?

**Oblomov**

I'll find it myself. I don't need a shirt anyway. See, I have my coat. It's warm enough—

**Zakhar**

Are you ill, Ilya?

**Oblomov**

Never better.

**Zakhar**

I thought I should never live to hear you talk like that.

**Oblomov**

I've changed.

**Zakhar**

You're beginning to sound like other people.

**Oblomov**

I'll make the bed myself. Get out. Dust later. Make us— (horrified, quickly correcting himself) me some biscuits for breakfast. Make a lot.

**Zakhar**

Anissya doesn't like to make biscuits for breakfast.

**Oblomov**

You make them, then.

**Zakhar**

But, I'm not the cook anymore.

**Oblomov**

Do it anyway.

**Zakhar**

But she'll be furious. She won't allow me to touch anything in HER kitchen.

**Oblomov**

Don't mind her.

**Zakhar**

I'd rather clean the place.

**Oblomov**

No.

**Zakhar**

But, I'm ready to clean, Ilya.

**Oblomov**

No.

**Zakhar**

But, it's so dirty.

**Oblomov**

You must be crazy; it doesn't need cleaning at all!

**Zakhar**

(throwing up his hands and dropping the mop and broom) Lord, how much longer am I to be punished like this?

**Oblomov**

Now, get out, and make some biscuits—with honey, mind you.

(Zakhar picks up the mop and broom and exits clumsily, knocking things over and bumping into things, cursing and talking to himself.)

**Olga**

(popping up) Ha, ha, ha.

**Oblomov**

Shh! You've got to get dressed before he comes back.

**Olga**

I'm fine like this.

**Oblomov**

But, you can't just stay there in bed all day!

**Olga**

Why not? You do. I'll keep you company.

**Oblomov**

But, this is scandalous.

**Olga**

What, staying in bed?

**Oblomov**

You are young and innocent. You don't realize how people would misunderstand the situation.

**Olga**

I think people would understand perfectly— They would assume we spent the night together and were having an affair—

**Oblomov**

People will talk.

**Olga**

Let them. We've better things to do.

**Oblomov**

But the danger is far greater than that. In the presence of an attractive woman, a man may lose his self control; his respect for purity and innocence is clouded, carried away in a whirlwind; swayed by passion, he no longer knows what he is doing—then—then—

**Olga**

And, then?

**Oblomov**

(shuddering at the horror of it) A fate worse than death for the woman.

**Olga**

You are clearly mad.

**Oblomov**

No, no, Olga—I am a man and I know— Promise me you will never sacrifice your precious honor—even if I beg you to do it.

**Olga**

(interrupting) Darling—

**Oblomov**

Yes, my love.

**Olga**

You have rather odd ideas—

**Oblomov**

You are such an innocent, Olga—people will think—you just don't understand—that we are having an affair.

**Olga**

(emphatically) We are having an affair.

**Oblomov**

It seems to me that is not quite the way to put it—

**Olga**

What did we do— (pointing to the bed) there last night—?

**Oblomov**

Last night?

**Olga**

Last night.

**Oblomov**

Why, nothing.

**Olga**

Nothing. It seems to me we did something.

**Oblomov**

That is an indelicate way to put it. I would rather say—

**Olga**

What do you prefer to say?

**Oblomov**

Err—nothing. Yes, I prefer to say nothing.

**Olga**

Doesn't your memory fail you sometimes? Because I fancy you don't remember what you do overnight?

**Oblomov**

(helplessly) Olga, my dear old friend. Olga—

**Olga**

Is that a jibe at my age?

**Oblomov**

No, no, of course not.

**Olga**

What did you do to me last night?

**Oblomov**

It wasn't that way.

**Olga**

(upset) What way was it?

**Oblomov**

Olga Sergeyevna, don't excite yourself, please.

**Olga**

Do you feel yourself confined?

**Oblomov**

No, no. (he could as easily have said, "Yes, yes")

**Olga**

Are you tired of me?

**Oblomov**

Certainly not.

**Olga**

Speak freely.

**Oblomov**

I—

**Olga**

Answer me with the same truth and sincerity I have answered you.

**Oblomov**

What is it I must answer you?

**Olga**

Speak from your soul.

**Oblomov**

Why am I asked so strange a question?

**Olga**

And to think, I want to marry a man like you?

**Oblomov**

How could a woman like you want to marry a man like me? Why make so strange a choice?

**Olga**

You make me impatient.

**Oblomov**

Marriage is a fine thing, a fine thing. But, I'd rather see my friends happy that way than myself. Marriage requires so much of one.

**Olga**

The dullest solitude is more pleasing to you than my company.

**Oblomov**

No, no.

**Olga**

My reputation—

**Oblomov**

Yes, about that, I think it would be better—

**Olga**

Reputation should always be sacred.

**Oblomov**

That is my opinion exactly, therefore—

**Olga**

I took you for quite another man.

**Oblomov**

What is it disturbs you?

**Olga**

Nothing—

**Oblomov**

The world will certainly report from false appearances, that I'm—

**Olga**

You don't love me—

**Oblomov**

Of course I do. Only let me love you in my own way. Quietly.

**Olga**

Secretly.

**Oblomov**

(wildly) You're the only person for whom I've made a journey. Can't you resign yourself to accepting me with all my infirmities—

**Olga**

I want to know if something actually happened last night—to me—to us—or if I was just dreaming.

**Oblomov**

It was like a dream to me.

**Olga**

You're incorrigible. (softening) Kiss me.

**Oblomov**

Now?

**Olga**

Now.

**Oblomov**

But, someone might come.

**Olga**

Let them.

**Oblomov**

Wouldn't it be better to wait?

**Olga**

You can be infuriating.

(They embrace. Suddenly, there is a thunderous knocking on the door.)

**Oblomov**

It's Tarantyev— Quick, under the blankets.

**Olga**

I'll never forgive you, if you hide me—if you're ashamed—

**Oblomov**

Please, Olga, I beg you—

**Olga**

Oh, very well. (she hides in the bed)

(Tarantyev stomps in; he is in a jovial mood.)

**Tarantyev**

Well friend, what about having a look at your new apartment?

**Oblomov**

That won't be necessary now. I—I—shan't be moving.

**Tarantyev**

(flabbergasted) Wha-at? What do you mean? You rented it, didn't you? What about the lease?

**Oblomov**

The lease?

**Tarantyev**

Forgotten, have you? You signed a lease for a year. Just give me the thousand roubles and you can go wherever you like.

**Oblomov**

But, I don't need an apartment. I'm going to Paris. I've promised Stolz to join him.

**Tarantyev**

With that Teuton? Not you! You'll never do it.

**Oblomov**

Oh no? I even have my passport and I've bought luggage.

**Tarantyev**

You won't go! You'd better let me have the rent for two months in advance.

**Oblomov**

But I haven't any money.

**Tarantyev**

Well, you can get it. I've already paid the landlady with my own money, so you can pay me.

**Oblomov**

Where did you get so much money?

**Tarantyev**

Is that your business? Give me the money!

**Oblomov**

Very well; in a few days I'll come and sublet the apartment, but just now, I'm in a hurry.

**Tarantyev**

You really ought to see it—very cozy—

**Oblomov**

I don't want to see it. Why should I move there? It's too far—

**Tarantyev**

From what?

**Oblomov**

(sighing to himself) From Olga Sergeyevna. (aloud) From the center.

**Tarantyev**

Eh? From the center of what? And why be near the center to lie in bed?

**Oblomov**

I don't lie in bed anymore.

**Tarantyev**

How is that?

**Oblomov**

I don't. Today, for example, I am dining out.

**Tarantyev**

Give me the money then, and go to the devil.

**Oblomov**

What money? I'll call at the apartment and talk it over with the landlady.

**Tarantyev**

The landlady? What does she know? You must talk to her brother. He'll give it to you. Just wait and see.

**Oblomov**

Very well. I'll talk with him.

**Tarantyev**

Better give me the money and let me manage him.

**Oblomov**

I told you I don't have it right now.

**Tarantyev**

(determined to get something out of him) Well, give me the money for my cab, at least.

**Oblomov**

How much?

**Tarantyev**

Three silver roubles.

**Oblomov**

Isn't that a lot?

**Tarantyev**

Well, it's a long drive.

**Oblomov**

Here—

**Tarantyev**

Now, give me the money for lunch.

**Oblomov**

Why lunch?

**Tarantyev**

Because, you've made me late, and I'll have to stop at a tavern—at least five silver roubles.

**Oblomov**

(anxious to get rid of him) Here.

**Tarantyev**

Tell Zakhar to give me something to eat.

**Oblomov**

But, I just paid for your lunch?

**Tarantyev**

Lunch, yes. But I want a snack.

**Oblomov**

Zakhar!

**Zakhar**

(entering cautiously) What now?

**Oblomov**

Have the cook make Tarantyev a snack.

**Tarantyev**

Some beef and a glass of wine.

**Zakhar**

No. Not until he returns your shirt and coat.

**Tarantyev**

What are you talking about? I returned them long ago.

**Zakhar**

When was that?

**Tarantyev**

I put them right in your hands. You stuck them in some bundle, and now you ask me for them—probably sold them for drink.

**Zakhar**

(hissing) I never in my life sold anything of my master's for drink. You—

**Oblomov**

Stop it, Zakhar.

**Zakhar**

You took a broom and two cups, too.

**Tarantyev**

Broom? What the hell are you talking about? You'd better get me something to eat before I get mad.

**Zakhar**

Never. There's no food in the house. And the cook is out. (he stalks off)

**Tarantyev**

Well, I'm damned. That's the influence of that damned Teuton!

**Oblomov**

(sharply)Tarantyev! Don't talk about what you don't understand.

**Tarantyev**

Such energy! Well then, I'm going. (he sees Oblomov's cap and puts it on) Lend me your cap, you don't wear it. (Tarantyev starts to leave and without a word Oblomov removes the cap from Tarantyev's head and places it on the bookstand; Tarantyev is completely nonplussed) Oh, the hell with you. (Tarantyev exits more puzzled than angry)

**Olga**

(popping out again) I've never been so humiliated in all my life!

**Oblomov**

But, Olga—

**Olga**

Making me hide like—like I don't know what—as if you were ashamed of me? Are you? (without waiting for an answer, Olga throws off the robe in a fury)

**Oblomov**

Olga Sergeyevna, what are you doing?

(Olga finds her clothes and, as rapidly as possible, proceeds to dress. Oblomov casts various conciliatory glances and gestures towards her, even begins several times to speak, but is cowed into silence by her scornful looks. Just as she is completing her toilet, Zakhar stomps in and stares speechlessly. Without a word, Olga storms past Zakhar and out of the house.)

**Oblomov**

Olga Sergeyevna, Olga Sergeyevna!

**Zakhar**

(softly) She's gone.

**Oblomov**

(in a daze) What?

**Zakhar**

She's gone.

(Oblomov regains control of himself and is now determined to make Zakhar deny his own senses.)

**Oblomov**

What are you talking about?

**Zakhar**

Olga Sergeyevna, of course.

**Oblomov**

Are you mad?

**Zakhar**

Huh?

**Oblomov**

There's no one here.

**Zakhar**

Eh? That's what I said. She just left.

**Oblomov**

No one just left.

**Zakhar**

I saw her myself. Two minutes ago. Less.

**Oblomov**

Are you seeing things?

**Zakhar**

I saw her with my own eyes.

**Oblomov**

Did she say anything to you?

**Zakhar**

No—uh. She just rushed out. All in a dither.

**Oblomov**

Is it likely she would do that?

**Zakhar**

(cagily) What do you mean?

**Oblomov**

If she had been here, wouldn't she have said, "Hello, Zakhar"?

**Zakhar**

Well she usually does.

**Oblomov**

Did she?

**Zakhar**

No. She didn't.

**Oblomov**

(with maddening reasonability) Then, how could she have been here?

**Zakhar**

But, I saw her.

**Oblomov**

You are seeing things.

**Zakhar**

But, I saw her.

**Oblomov**

(threateningly) If you continue to see such things, I shall have to send you away, Zakhar I can't have servants that see things—

**Zakhar**

(comprehending) Perhaps, I was mistaken—

**Oblomov**

Of course you were— (Zakhar starts to leave) Zakhar.

**Zakhar**

What is it?

**Oblomov**

Where has the money gone? We've almost nothing left.

**Zakhar**

Do I know where you spend your money?

**Oblomov**

If only you had written it down.

**Zakhar**

I've lived my life without knowing how to read or write, what of it? You probably spent it on preparations for the wedding.

**Oblomov**

What wedding?

**Zakhar**

Yours, of course.

**Oblomov**

Me? Getting married? To whom?

**Zakhar**

To Olga Sergeyevna.

**Oblomov**

(advancing) Who put that in your head, you miserable wretch?

**Zakhar**

Why am I a miserable wretch?

**Oblomov**

Not another word.

**Zakhar**

Did I invent it? Miss Olga's servant told cook, and cook told me.

**Oblomov**

(low) So. Even the servants are talking. This is what it has come to. (aloud) How did you know—err, I mean what makes you think I am getting married?

**Zakhar**

Vasilisa told Anissya and Anissya told me.

**Oblomov**

(sternly) Zakhar!

**Zakhar**

Yes, sir.

**Oblomov**

Come here!

**Zakhar**

(not coming) Do you want me to fetch something?

**Oblomov**

Come here!

**Zakhar**

(not budging) There's no room. I can hear fine from where I am.

**Oblomov**

Closer.

**Zakhar**

(not moving) This is as far as I can go. (aside) Aiee! I'm in for it now.

**Oblomov**

How could you ask me such a venomous question?

**Zakhar**

I'd better call Anissya.

**Oblomov**

I want to speak to you, not the cook. Why did you invent such a story?

**Zakhar**

(stubbornly) I did not invent it.

**Oblomov**

It's a lie, do you hear? (pause) It cannot be.

**Zakhar**

Why can't it be? Lots of other people get married.

**Oblomov**

There you go, again, comparing me to other people. Are you listening to me? What is a wedding?

**Zakhar**

A wedding is a wedding—when people get married.

**Oblomov**

Listen, I'll explain to you. A wedding is when dozens of idle people buzz around. A wedding is constant rehearsals and dressing up in fancy clothes that don't fit right because they are rented— Do you dare to suggest that I could endure that?

**Zakhar**

Well, you'd only have to do it once. Can I go?

**Oblomov**

Stay here. You have forgotten all the confusion, the running about—the unwelcome guests— In short, weddings are—work.

**Zakhar**

Shall I call Anissya?

**Oblomov**

(puzzled) What for?

**Zakhar**

(fingering prayer beads) What have I done to deserve such punishment?

**Oblomov**

And the expense? What about the expense? I have no money left. And, I have to settle up for the apartment Tarantyev rented— How could I get married?

**Zakhar**

Other people with your income—less—get married.

**Oblomov**

Other people again! Take care! Other people live in one room and have only one maid to do the housework and the wife to do the shopping. Do you imagine Olga Sergeyevna could go to the—market?

**Zakhar**

Well, I could do that. Besides, she's got bundles of money.

**Oblomov**

Don't you see how fatiguing it would all be— (he breaks off into an agonized revery)

(Zakhar waits patiently, afraid that if he leaves he will be called back, although he starts to leave several times, but thinks better of it.)

**Oblomov**

(ending his trance) Well, what is it?

**Zakhar**

Well, you told me to stand here—

**Oblomov**

Go—

(Zakhar obediently starts to leave.)

**Oblomov**

Wait!

**Zakhar**

Here we go again!

**Oblomov**

How did you dare to spread such a venomous rumor about me?

**Zakhar**

(hurt) When did I spread it, Ilya Ilyich? Somebody told me, that's all.

**Oblomov**

Not a word—ever— Do you hear?

**Zakhar**

Yes, sir. (leaving again)

**Oblomov**

Zakhar! (Zakhar stops in his tracks without turning) Look at this dirt! You'd better dust and sweep again. Olga Sergeyevna gives me no peace. "You must like dirt," she says. I thought I told you to sweep first thing.

**Zakhar**

(almost, but not quite speechless, staring reproachfully) It's all very well for her to talk. She has five servants.

**Oblomov**

Well, why don't you start sweeping? What are you standing there for?

(Zakhar helplessly begins to putter around and suddenly triumphantly brings up a lady's unmentionable.)

**Zakhar**

Ha, ha. ha.

## CURTAIN

# ACT III
## SCENE 5: Oblomov's Room in Madame Pshenitsyn's House

*The room is furnished with Oblomov's furniture, but rearranged. We can tell from the presence of a balcony that we are in a different house. Everything is neat and clean; not a speck of dust. Enter Tarantyev and Madame Pshenitsyn.*

**Tarantyev**

I wonder where he can have gone?

**Madame**

Oh, sometimes, he's in the garden hammock.

**Tarantyev**

Well, do I deserve my reward?

**Madame**

Yes, if he stays.

**Tarantyev**

He'll stay.

**Madame**

Still—

**Tarantyev**

Let's have a drink.

(Madame Pshenitsyn pours from a decanter. They both drink.)

**Tarantyev**

To Oblomov.

**Madame**

To Oblomovism.

**Tarantyev**

This is good stuff, what is it?

**Madame**

Real Jamaica Rum. (she offers more, he accepts)

**Tarantyev**

You must admit I deserve a treat. The house might have rotted and never seen a lodger like this.

**Madame**

That's so, that's so.

**Tarantyev**

And, if it comes off, and you marry him—

**Madame**

I am afraid he may be leaving. He keeps saying it's only temporary—

**Tarantyev**

Where will he go? A woman like you ought to have more sense! You'd have to drive him away by force. They couldn't get rid of him where he was before. He stayed there ten years—temporarily.

**Madame**

But they say his is going to marry.

**Tarantyev**

Marry! Why, he can't go to sleep without Zakhar's help. How could he marry? He doesn't know what's what.

**Madame**

Still—he is so—attractive.

**Tarantyev**

(puzzled) What woman would be attracted to a pitiful, helpless thing like that?

**Madame**

That's exactly what makes him so—exciting—his helplessness.

**Tarantyev**

Bah! Not a man.

**Madame**

All I am afraid of is his marriage to Miss Olga.

**Tarantyev**

Don't worry. It will come to nothing, I tell you.

**Madame**

But, she's so bold. I can't keep up with shamelessness like that. (gaily) Do you know he is casting sheep's eyes at yours truly?

**Tarantyev**

Already? You don't say so!

**Madame**

Don't you let on.

**Tarantyev**

I wouldn't have dreamed it. And, how do you feel about it?

**Madame**

(serenely) Oh—you know me.

**Tarantyev**

Just think what it may lead to—

**Madame**

He's always asking to see my brother—

**Tarantyev**

He never will.

**Madame**

As I haven't got one. He intended to leave and break the lease. But, as he had to see my brother—and as my brother has never been around, he's been here four months.

**Tarantyev**

Did he ask about me?

**Madame**

I told him you were a friend of my brother—

(They both laugh. Oblomov returns.)

**Oblomov**

Ah, Tarantyev. I was just about to lie down—an afternoon siesta.

**Tarantyev**

Good day, friend.

**Oblomov**

(gallantly) Ah, Madame Pshenitsyn. How peaceful and happy you look.

**Tarantyev**

(with feeling) This woman is a perfect jewel, as I told you.

**Oblomov**

You're quite right. Quite right. A diamond. Madame Pshenitsyn, has your brother come round lately?

**Madame**

No. He's still away.

**Oblomov**

I'd really like to meet him.

**Madame**

Is it the pigs or the chickens that are bothering you?

**Oblomov**

No, no. I pay them no heed.

**Madame**

The chickens make a frightful racket and the pigs smell awfully. We will take them further off—

**Oblomov**

That doesn't matter either—but I can't stay indefinitely.

**Madame**

As you please. But my brother will make you pay compensation— A whole year's rent.

**Oblomov**

That's unfair.

**Madame**

But my brother is very exact. He told me it was in the contract.

**Oblomov**

Surely, you can persuade your brother—

**Madame**

He never listens to me. You must speak to him yourself.

**Oblomov**

But, he never comes—

**Madame**

But he's away on business—and I can do nothing without him—Well, I must attend to my work— (she leaves)

**Oblomov**

She is a jewel.

**Tarantyev**

I thought you might like to go to the Park?

**Oblomov**

Whatever for?

**Tarantyev**

Well, there'll be fireworks. I love fireworks.

**Oblomov**

Fireworks is not very exciting. Besides I have work to do.

**Tarantyev**

I'll stop back in a while for dinner.

**Oblomov**

Good. I don't get much company out here.

(Tarantyev exits. Oblomov looks longingly at the bed, but decides, after an agonizing struggle, against it. He sees a bowl of coffee and pours it into a cup and drinks. He tries to look at some papers, yawns, puts them aside, sips more coffee, looks back at the bed.)

**Oblomov**

Zakhar!

**Zakhar**

Sir?

**Oblomov**

What excellent coffee. Did Anissya make it?

**Zakhar**

Could Anissya do anything right? The landlady, of course.

**Oblomov**

Go thank her for me.

(Zakhar goes out. Oblomov moves from one seat to the armchair. Still casting avid glances at the bed, he takes up first a paper, then a book, yawns as he casts them aside. But he steels himself, smothers a yawn and continues to read. Olga, looking well, but somewhat perturbed enters. She is wearing a riding cloak.)

**Oblomov**

(startled, looks up) You here?

**Olga**

You are well! You're not in bed!

**Oblomov**

My health is almost back to normal.

**Olga**

Why didn't you come yesterday?

**Oblomov**

(confused) Yesterday. Well, that is to say—

**Olga**

(furious) I'm waiting.

**Oblomov**

But, Olga—do you realize what you are doing, coming here? My landlady—

**Olga**

We'll discuss that later! I ask you: what is the meaning of your staying away?

(Oblomov makes no reply.)

**Olga**

Was your throat sore, like the last time?

**Oblomov**

(after saying nothing at first) No. (timidly) You see, Olga—

**Olga**

You have deceived me. Why?

**Oblomov**

I'll explain everything, Olga. An important reason forced me to stay away for two weeks— I was afraid—

**Olga**

Of what?

**Oblomov**

(under his breath) You. (aloud) Talk. Gossip.

**Olga**

But, you weren't afraid of my spending nights alone, thinking God knows what!

**Oblomov**

You don't know what is going on—

**Olga**

What's going on?

**Oblomov**

The rumors about us.

**Olga**

That is bourgeois.

**Oblomov**

I didn't want to alarm you. I was afraid to face you.

**Olga**

That, too, is bourgeois. Never mind. (brightening up, she is glad to see him) We must announce our marriage. Then, there will be no more rumors. (smiling) When will we be married?

**Oblomov**

(uneasily) Soon.

**Olga**

If I didn't know you to be the most honest man in the world, and terribly in love with me, I might suspect you were trying to get rid of me.

**Oblomov**

No, no—Olga. Never think it. I worship you. I only thought the talk would upset you.

**Olga**

But I've known about it all along.

**Oblomov**

You're known?

**Olga**

Of course. I've already been congratulated many times by my servants.

**Oblomov**

But, this is horrible.

**Olga**

But the rumors are not without foundation, are they?

**Oblomov**

No, no. Of course not. But, I thought if I stayed away— I was hoping they'd quiet down— I was afraid—

**Olga**

Afraid! You're trembling like a little boy. I, on the other hand, am not easily upset by trifles.

**Oblomov**

But, is your reputation a trifle?

**Olga**

What a man to have an affair with, really.

**Oblomov**

I'm hopeless, I know it. I'm not up to these love affairs. I worry about everything.

**Olga**

(amused) Why not worry about me? (she smiles mischievously and takes off her cloak) What have you been doing all this time?

**Oblomov**

(sincerely) Reading, writing— Mostly thinking about you.

**Olga**

(examining the book) The pages are uncut— You haven't been reading.

**Oblomov**

(faltering) There was so little time. In the morning, they tidy up the rooms—which is disturbing—then there's dinner. When is there time to read?

**Olga**

(flatly) You slept after lunch?

**Oblomov**

(guiltily) Usually.

**Olga**

(imperiously) Why?

**Oblomov**

So I wouldn't notice the time. You were not with me, and life is so dull, unbearable, without you—

**Olga**

You are sliding back. You have deceived me!

**Oblomov**

Deceived you! Do you doubt my love? I would make any sacrifice—

**Olga**

But, who is asking you to make any special sacrifice?

**Oblomov**

You don't know what all this passion has done to my health! I have had no other thought since I met you. You are the aim of my life. Is it any wonder that when I don't see you, I give up and fall asleep?

**Olga**

(laughing) Oh, it's impossible to be angry with you! (walking about) What a depressing place this is. The windows are so small (shutting the blinds) The wallpaper so old. (beginning to disrobe)

**Oblomov**

Yes, it really is a terrible place. But, it's only temporary. Only temporary. (he sees what she is doing) Good God, Olga, you can't—

**Olga**

Why not?

**Oblomov**

It's the middle of the afternoon.

**Olga**

So? One time's as good as another.

**Oblomov**

But, my landlady— (picking up her clothes as she sheds them)

**Olga**

To hell with your landlady. Lock the door. (Olga is now in her chemise and lying on the couch) I miss you. (he locks the door)

**Oblomov**

But, Olga—

**Olga**

Haven't you missed me?

**Oblomov**

Of course, of course. Terribly.

**Olga**

(languorously) Then, come here.

**Oblomov**

But Tarantyev may be back any minute.

**Olga**

(furious) Why did you invite him?

**Oblomov**

You see, he's going to help me.

**Olga**

(getting up and dressing in a rage) What do you need his help for?

**Oblomov**

My estate is in disorder again. I'll give him a power of attorney. That way I don't have to go there myself. (coaxingly) I won't have to leave you. I couldn't bear it. (Olga is slightly mollified) You see, I'm not used to traveling. And even if I did go, I wouldn't know what to do— If only Stolz would come back.

**Olga**

Yes, Stolz is a real man. (Meaning Oblomov is not. The irony is lost on Oblomov. Olga finishes dressing and opens the windows. She looks out the window for a while, then softens.) Poor darling. You're not very good at the administrative side of love, are you?

**Oblomov**

I—Olga—you are not angry?

**Olga**

Oh, what's the use? When we are married, we can stay in bed

all day.

**Oblomov**

(shudders) Yes, my dear.

**Olga**

When will we be married?

**Oblomov**

(uneasily) Soon.

**Olga**

Darling, I meant to tell you. We shouldn't delay much longer.

**Oblomov**

No—no—only until this business with my estate is settled.

**Olga**

Because—how long will that take?

**Oblomov**

Oh, perhaps, a year.

**Olga**

A year!

**Oblomov**

Until then, we mustn't see each other like this too often.

**Olga**

(sitting down) A whole year—but, in six months—

**Oblomov**

Eh?

**Olga**

Nothing. Nothing at all. Why must we wait a year to put your estate in order?

**Oblomov**

Because I may have no money. Everything is such a mess. Olga—we can't marry—

**Olga**

I see. (pause) (in a low voice) And in six months—

**Oblomov**

In six months?

**Olga**

Nothing.

(Zakhar attempts to enter; Oblomov blocks his entrance.)

**Zakhar**

I thanked her.

**Oblomov**

Zakhar, the other day you asked to go visit your cousin. Well, you can go—now.

**Zakhar**

Today? No, tomorrow would be better.

**Oblomov**

Go, and have a good time.

**Zakhar**

Who goes visiting on a weekday? I won't go.

**Oblomov**

Yes, you will.

**Zakhar**

But, I can't have a good time on a weekday.

**Oblomov**

Nonsense—go on.

**Zakhar**

No—I'm staying home all day today. But, I might go Sunday.

**Oblomov**

(in great agitation) Go now! At once!

**Zakhar**

Why should I go all that distance?

**Oblomov**

Go for a walk, then—look at your face. You need fresh air.

**Zakhar**

I'd rather sit on the front steps—

**Oblomov**

Here's money—go have some Vodka.

**Zakhar**

That's very kind of you, Ilya, but I'd rather sit on the front steps.

**Oblomov**

You will not sit on the steps. I will not allow you to sit on the steps.

**Zakhar**

Well, I'll sit by the gate then.

**Oblomov**

If you don't want the day off, go to the market.

**Zakhar**

But, I just went to the market this morning.

**Oblomov**

Go, again.

**Zakhar**

But, it's a long way.

**Oblomov**

Be quiet and listen. I want you to buy some asparagus.

**Zakhar**

Asparagus is out of season.— Where would I find it?

**Oblomov**

Look very hard. Run as fast as you can—and don't look back.

**Zakhar**

(going out) What a plague!

**Oblomov**

(exhausted) What a venomous man. Well, at least I got rid of him.

**Olga**

Yes. Now we can—

**Oblomov**

(apprehensively looking at the bed) Of course.

**Olga**

—talk.

**Oblomov**

(visibly relieved) Certainly, certainly.

**Olga**

There's something I must ask you.

**Oblomov**

(amiably What is it?

**Olga**

Do you like children?

**Oblomov**

Of course I like children.

**Olga**

I mean, do you want to be a father?

**Oblomov**

Me? A father! What an incredible idea? What would I do with children? I mean they make noise, and they're so dirty, and—

**Olga**

I see.

**Oblomov**

I really don't.

**Olga**

There's something I must tell you.

**Oblomov**

What is it?

**Olga**

It's rather important.

**Oblomov**

Well?

(Oblomov quits his post at the door and Tarantyev enters. Olga and Oblomov spring apart.)

**Tarantyev**

I must have dropped some money here, brother. Did you find five silver roubles?

**Oblomov**

Good God!

**Tarantyev**

Olga Sergeyevna. (bowing)

**Olga**

Good day, Mr. Tarantyev.

**Tarantyev**

Fancy meeting you here.

**Olga**

I came to visit Mr. Oblomov, who I heard was ill.

**Tarantyev**

Him, ill?

**Olga**

It was just a lie someone told me.

**Tarantyev**

The rumors people spread nowadays.

**Olga**

I am just going. (slyly) You must call on us, Mr. Tarantyev.

**Tarantyev**

(preening like a peacock) Tomorrow, if I may.

**Olga**

(frowning) Certainly, I shall expect you. (firmly) Goodbye, Mr. Oblomov. (exits)

**Oblomov**

(in agony) Please don't misunderstand. She was concerned for my health. Don't mention seeing her here.

**Tarantyev**

Seeing who here? There's no one here.

**Oblomov**

Thank you.

**Tarantyev**

Now, if I could only find that ten roubles I lost here. Lend it to me, Ilya. It will turn up eventually.

**Oblomov**

(prostrated) Gladly, gladly.

**SHORT CURTAIN OR BLACKOUT**

# ACT III

SCENE 6: THE SAME, NEXT MORNING

*Zakhar is clearing up a bit. Oblomov is in the armchair. Zakhar picks up a woman's—well, Goncharov said it was a woman's glove. Perhaps Olga had an odd shaped hand.*

**Zakhar**

Olga Sergeyevna must have left this.

**Oblomov**

Devil! Nothing of the sort! (rising) What are you talking about? It was a dressmaker who came to fit my shirts. How dare you invent such stories.

**Zakhar**

Why devil? What am I inventing? They are saying downstairs that—

**Oblomov**

What?

**Zakhar**

Why, Olga Sergeyevna was here—

**Oblomov**

And, how should they know? You and Anissya must have gossiped—

**Zakhar**

(indignant) I did not—

**Oblomov**

Get out, you venomous creature— (Deeply wounded, Zakhar leaves. Oblomov paces briefly, then resumes his seat in the armchair. Enter Madame Pshenitsyn. She resembles a plump doll that cries "mama" and "papa". She is pretty, affable, and totally unaware of the effect she has on men. She wears a shawl that covers her ample bosom, but occasionally slides loose.)

**Madame**

I've been darning your socks today.

**Oblomov**

(rising) How kind of you.

**Madame**

It's nothing. It's my job to look after things. You have no one to sort them for you.

**Oblomov**

Just throw them away. Why should you spend your time on such rubbish? I can buy new ones.

**Madame**

Throw them away! But, why? These can be mended.

**Oblomov**

Do sit down, please. Why do you stand?

**Madame**

No, thank you. This is our wash day. I must get the clothes ready.

**Oblomov**

(with his eyes fixed on her neck and bosom) You're a wonder, not a housekeeper.

**Madame**

Well, then, shall I darn the socks?

**Oblomov**

(still cannot take his eyes off her) Since you are so kind, it would be a great favor; but I am really ashamed to give you so much trouble.

**Madame**

Not at all—

**Oblomov**

I don't know how to thank you—

**Madame**

That's all right. (starting to leave)

**Oblomov**

Why are you in such a hurry? Do sit down. (practically pushing her into a chair) Stay a little. (pause) Listen, my servants talk a lot of nonsense, but don't believe them, for Heaven's sake.

**Madame**

What are they saying?

**Oblomov**

They are saying that a young lady comes to visit me.

**Madame**

It's none of our business what visitors our tenants may have, is it?

**Oblomov**

Don't believe it. It isn't a young lady at all. Just a dressmaker that is making some shirts for me.

**Madame**

But it's all right for you to have visitors.

**Oblomov**

(hotly) It was a dressmaker!

**Madame**

But, it makes no difference. (rising) Anyway, I have to go.

**Oblomov**

(coyly, holding her in the chair) What if I won't let you?

**Madame**

(easily, not disconcerted) Please, let me go. I have to prepare dinner.

**Oblomov**

(distracted by the thought of dinner) What are we having?

**Madame**

Salmon—your favorite.

**Oblomov**

Excellent. You always remember what I like.

**Madame**

And, what am I here for?

**Oblomov**

You should get married.

**Madame**

And, who would marry me, with two children?

**Oblomov**

Lots of men, lots of men. (very gallant) I've noticed how pretty you are— I can't help noticing—

**Madame**

Mr. Oblomov—

**Oblomov**

Tell me, what if I fell in love with you—?

**Madame**

(smiling a Mona Lisa smile) Pish—

**Oblomov**

Would you love me?

**Madame**

Why not? God commanded us to love everyone.

**Oblomov**

And if I stole a kiss?

**Madame**

Take care— (Oblomov kisses her lightly on the cheek. Madame

shows no embarrassment, but stands like a horse when its collar is being put on.)

**Madame**

Do you still want to see my brother about cancelling the lease?

**Oblomov**

No. (hoarsely) I, I shall stay longer—than I intended. It's very—cozy—and restful here.

**Madame**

I really must get back to my kitchen. (darting out) (Zakhar enters. He is still upset.)

**Oblomov**

What do you want?

**Zakhar**

A visitor for you.

**Oblomov**

Who is it? Tarantyev or Alekseyev?

**Zakhar**

Mr. Stolz.

**Oblomov**

Stolz? Good Heavens, what will he say when he sees—? (looking around for a way out) Tell him, I have gone out. (Enter Stolz.)

**Stolz**

Have I disturbed you?

**Oblomov**

(uneasily) Where are you coming from? How did you find me? How long are you staying?

**Stolz**

Finding you was easy. But, I shan't stay more than a few days.

**Oblomov**

(a little relieved) Ahh—

**Stolz**

(sternly) Well, Ilya? (pause) Then, it's never.

**Oblomov**

What do you mean, never?

**Stolz**

You have forgotten "now or never".

**Oblomov**

I am not the same now as I was then.

**Stolz**

Why didn't you join me in Paris?

**Oblomov**

I was—prevented.

**Stolz**

Olga? That's wonderful. When is the wedding?

**Oblomov**

No, no. You mustn't say that. We're not—

**Stolz**

She turned you down?

**Oblomov**

Not, no, that is to say—

**Stolz**

Did you make an offer?

**Oblomov**

No. No, I didn't.

**Stolz**

No. Hmmm. Are you unhappy?

**Oblomov**

(honestly) No. It's better this way.

**Stolz**

You're letting me down, old boy. As for Olga—

**Oblomov**

Don't speak of it. Don't recall it. It's over. I was not worthy of so energetic a woman. I knew it from the beginning. If I've caused her pain— The thought that I've made her suffer is a burden to me.

**Stolz**

You really are a soul as clear as crystal.

**Oblomov**

It is quiet and restful here. No one disturbs me in my work.

**Stolz**

(astonished) What work?

**Oblomov**

Oh, I've almost completed my five year plan for reorganizing my estate.

**Stolz**

Well, now there is nothing to prevent you from joining me in Paris. Let us go next week.

**Oblomov**

But all my belongings are here. I can't go just like that.

**Stolz**

You don't take your furniture on a trip.

**Oblomov**

My health isn't what it used to be—

**Stolz**

You must come to yourself, Ilya. I will not leave you in peace.

**Oblomov**

Life!

**Stolz**

What about it?

**Oblomov**

It disturbs one, gives a body no peace. I wish I could lie down and sleep forever—

**Stolz**

Fine sort of life! You want to put the light out and remain in darkness. Oh, I wish I could live two or three hundred years! How much one could do then!

**Oblomov**

You are different. You have wings, you fly! You are not fat, the back of your head doesn't itch.

**Stolz**

Nonsense! Man was created to arrange life for himself. You had wings once, but you cut them off.

**Oblomov**

(pathetically) Where are they, those wings? I don't know how to do anything.

**Stolz**

You don't want to know! There isn't a man living who can't do something.

**Oblomov**

There's me.

**Stolz**

You can do it.

**Oblomov**

There's no going back.

**Stolz**

Go forward.

**Oblomov**

No, I can't go forward either. I'm stuck—right where I am.

**Stolz**

What shall I tell Olga?

**Oblomov**

Say you haven't seen me.

**Stolz**

She won't believe that.

**Oblomov**

Tell her I'm dead.

**Stolz**

I can't do that.

**Oblomov**

For all practical purposes—

**Stolz**

Do you mean what I think you mean?

**Oblomov**

Ah—yes. (Enter Madame Pshenitsyn.)

**Madame**

I just thought you might want some more dessert, Ilya dear.

**Oblomov**

Katrinka, you shouldn't.

**Madame**

Never mind. (she puts the desert down) I've got to go. (she curtsies to Stolz) My stove is waiting. (Stolz watches this exchange with growing wonder.)

**Stolz**

All right. I'll tell Olga. She'll be hurt. I'll lie to her. I'll say you're living on memories of her. And I'll say nothing about Katrinka?

**Oblomov**

What do you mean?

**Stolz**

You know very well, or you wouldn't be blushing. I am beginning to think you love her.

**Oblomov**

What next?

**Stolz**

Mind you don't fall into the pit. An uneducated woman.

**Oblomov**

And, why does one need an educated woman, may I ask?

**Stolz**

Ilya.

**Oblomov**

What good are they?

**Stolz**

You speak with such heat.

**Oblomov**

What are you talking about?

**Stolz**

I see what's happening.

**Oblomov**

Nothing's happening.

**Stolz**

Goodbye, Ilya.

**Oblomov**

Goodbye. (Stolz leaves. After a moment Tarantyev enters.)

**Tarantyev**

How do you do, neighbor? Have you said goodbye to your benefactor?

**Oblomov**

You still don't like him?

**Tarantyev**

I should like to hang him!

**Oblomov**

What for?

**Tarantyev**

Isn't he trying to persuade you to leave? I have settled you here, I've found a perfect treasure of a woman for you! I've assured peace and comfort for you, I've simply showered benefits on you, and you turn your back on me for that Teuton.

**Oblomov**

Don't worry, I'm staying. I think I will go lie in the garden hammock. (Oblomov goes out, Madame comes in a moment later.)

**Madame**

I don't like this German.

**Tarantyev**

Yes, the devil brought him back.

**Madame**

He will take my Oblomov away— (blubbering)

**Tarantyev**

You are too easily scared. The German may be angry and shout—Germans always do—but Oblomov will never leave now.

**Madame**

(cheering up) Is that so? Well, let's have a little vodka. (goes to table and pours)

**Tarantyev**

Meanwhile, I'll tell you what I must do—

**Madame**

No—I'll tell you.

**Tarantyev**

Well?

**Madame**

He comes to my room very often— You speak to him and say it isn't right to bring disgrace upon a family—tell him that people are talking—that I had a suitor—a rich merchant, but now that he has heard about Oblomov spending his time with me, he has backed out—

**Tarantyev**

Well, what then? He will be frightened, get into bed, sigh—and turn from side to side like a pig, that's all. What's the advantage?

**Madame**

You will see; he hates a scandal.

**Tarantyev**

I called on Olga Sergeyevna. I believe she likes me.

**Madame**

And, why not? Many women like a man who is a little—uncouth.

**Tarantyev**

And, if I should marry her—what a catch!

**Madame**

Go to her.

**Tarantyev**

I shall make her an offer.

**Madame**

Do—

**Tarantyev**

I will.

**BLACKOUT**

# ACT III
## SCENE 7: OBLOMOV'S BEDROOM, ABOUT EIGHT MONTHS LATER

*It is the same room, but it has undergone some changes. The bed has moved into the central position. It has somewhat the appearance of a sickroom, or at any rate of a room from which the occupant is never absent. Everything has been sacrificed to comfort. Soft pillows line the chairs. Oblomov lies propped up in bed, stuffed between massive pillows. He is in his dressing gown. Madame Pshenitsyn sits by him spooning soup into his mouth.*

**Madame**

Do you like it, my Ilya?

**Oblomov**

It's delicious.

**Madame**

It's my special recipe. (she dips out a spoonful more)

**Oblomov**

Mmm!

**Madame**

Wait a minute, I'll give you fish. The best sturgeon.

**Oblomov**

Don't trouble yourself. (he slurps his food and Madame wipes his chin)! Zakhar! Zakhar! (Zakhar reels in, staggering drunk.)

**Zakhar**

(in mock English accent) You rang, sir!

**Oblomov**

(shocked) Zakhar, you're drunk. You should be ashamed of yourself. It's the middle of the day, too.

**Zakhar**

I didn't invent drunkenness. Why shouldn't I be drunk? I have nothing to do. (pointing accusingly at Madame) SHE does everything for you. I don't even get to pull off your boots anymore. (weeping)

**Oblomov**

But Zakhar, I never get out of bed. Do you expect me to wear boots in bed?

**Zakhar**

You never even order me to sweep up, either.

**Oblomov**

But Madame keeps the place spotless.

**Zakhar**

So, why shouldn't I be drunk? Being drunk doesn't prevent me from doing nothing—'cos I have nothing to do.

**Oblomov**

Please go fetch a pie from the kitchen.

**Zakhar**

But I'm drunk. How can you ask a drunk to go fetch a pie? It's unreasonable.

**Oblomov**

Fetch it now!

**Zakhar**

(aside) Now, that's what I like to hear. (aloud, grumbling) When am I to be released from this misery, Lord? (he staggers off, delighted) (Enter Alekseyev.)

**Alekseyev**

Greetings, Ilya.

**Oblomov**

Ah, Alekseyev. Glad you've come. You're just in time for lunch.

**Alekseyev**

Well, I can't eat.

**Oblomov**

But, the food's delicious—

**Alekseyev**

All the more reason, I'm on a diet. Greetings, Madame Pshenitsyn.

**Madame**

Greetings, Mr. Alekseyev.

**Oblomov**

Tell me something.

**Alekseyev**

There's nothing to tell.

**Oblomov**

How can that be? You go to people—to visit.

**Alekseyev**

Well, nothing much. Madame Tarantyev has had a baby.

**Oblomov**

A baby?

**Alekseyev**

Yes. Sleepy little fellow. I expect Tarantyev will be by to brag about it.

**Oblomov**

Oh—I'm so glad to hear there was a safe delivery.

**Alekseyev**

Olga Sergeyevna is fine. But she's been awfully bad tempered since she got married.

**Oblomov**

I am sorry she's not at ease.

**Alekseyev**

She gives that lout Tarantyev what for. I saw them together the other day. She marches him about like a drill sergeant.

**Oblomov**

I'm sure she would do that to any man. (aside) There, but for the grace of God—

**Alekseyev**

She's been spending most of her time in bed recently. You two have a lot in common.

**Oblomov**

(uneasily) Oh, I think not. (changing the subject) Let's talk about politics—what's the news?

**Alekseyev**

Oh, the English have recalled their Ambassador.

**Oblomov**

To what country?

**Alekseyev**

To Spain or Turkey, I think.

**Oblomov**

I suppose it makes little difference. (Zakhar returns with the pie. He is still drunk. He clumsily places the pie on the table near Madame.)

**Oblomov**

Go set a place for Mr. Alekseyev.

**Zakhar**

(aside) Ah. That's more like it. (aloud) What next?

(Zakhar goes out. A thunderous noise is heard. Alekseyev cringes.)

**Oblomov**

It must be Tarantyev.

**Tarantyev**

(entering) Good morning, friend, good morning. Well, you look as though you were well cared for. Madame Pshenitsyn. (bowing)

**Oblomov**

Everything is just perfect. I need hardly move. Madame is a wonder. She sees to my every comfort.

**Tarantyev**

You see. I knew it would suit you perfectly. And you wanted to move away.

**Oblomov**

That would have been a great mistake. I like it here.

**Tarantyev**

Well, I am a father—how about that? A bouncing baby boy. I've named him Ilya, after you.

**Oblomov**

(uneasily) That's very kind.

**Tarantyev**

Cute little mite. Looks just like his mother. But he sleeps all the time—never seen a baby so—torpid.

**Oblomov**

Then he is well named. (pause) Why don't you offer Alekseyev a cigar?

**Tarantyev**

Eh? Is that sniveling creature here? Sorry—didn't see you—have a cigar in honor of my child.

**Madame**

Oh dear, dear. I almost forgot the meat. (she rushes off)

**Tarantyev**

Yes, that's virility for you. One turn in the hay—and she's pregnant. It takes a real man to do that.

**Alekseyev**

Don't boast.

**Tarantyev**

Silence, weasel! And tell that cousin of yours to stop writing me letters.

**Alekseyev**

I told you before, I have no cousin.

**Tarantyev**

A likely story. Tell him, if he keeps it up, I'll throttle him—like this— (he squeezes Alekseyev by the neck till he turns red, then purple) Just like that. (Enter Stolz.)

**Oblomov**

Is it you, Stolz? (Tarantyev releases Alekseyev and makes a gesture of distaste.)

**Stolz**

It's me. Are you well?

**Oblomov**

In the very pink of health.

**Stolz**

But, why are you like that?

**Oblomov**

Oh, my landlady pampers me.

**Stolz**

Why didn't you follow me to Paris, as you promised?

**Oblomov**

What am I to tell you? You know me and you mustn't ask.

**Stolz**

And you just lay in bed?

**Oblomov**

My landlady occasionally rolls the bed into the garden in the summer.

**Stolz**

Good heavens, you can't stay like this.

**Oblomov**

Why not?

**Stolz**

It's unnatural.

**Oblomov**

Don't speak so loud; she might hear you.

**Stolz**

Who?

**Oblomov**

My landlady.

**Stolz**

What of it? Let her.

**Oblomov**

Oh, no. She might actually think I meant to leave.

**Stolz**

You're done for, Ilya. Come to your senses.

**Oblomov**

But, I have. Why try to change one's nature? I'm happy this way.

**Stolz**

But, what about your dreams?

**Oblomov**

But, I still have them. I dream all day. Seriously, Stolz, don't disturb the past. Don't remind me. I have grown into this little world. Forcibly tear me from it and I will perish like an uprooted tree.

**Stolz**

Is this you, Ilya? You favor your landlady over me— What is that woman to you?

**Oblomov**

She is my wife.

**Stolz**

I'll arrange an annulment.

**Oblomov**

What for? We are very happy.

**Tarantyev**

Why don't you just leave him alone? Can't you see he's happy this way? Go back to Germany and work all day long. We Russians have better things to do.

**Stolz**

I'm leaving—and I won't come back. But, we're still friends, Ilya?

**Oblomov**

Of course—I love you still. I just can't take your way. (Stolz embraces Oblomov with tears in his eyes. Tarantyev makes disparaging gestures unseen by either Oblomov or Stolz.)

**Oblomov**

Goodbye, friend of my youth. (Stolz hurries out.)

**Tarantyev**

At last, now we'll have some peace over here. (going towards the door) (Madame Oblomov enters with a meat dish.)

(to Madame) You're a saint to endure this. How do you manage?

**Madame**

(smiling) Oh, we know how to care for our guests. (Zakhar returns)

**Zakhar**

(to Tarantyev) You. When are you going to return those trousers?

**Tarantyev**

(aiming a kick at Zakhar) Are you at it, again? I returned them. (to Oblomov) By the way, Ilya, can I use your watch? You don't need it. (Oblomov is about to reply, but Madame Oblomov spoons some meat into his mouth.)

**Madame**

Is it good, darling? See how mumsie takes care of her dear one.

(Tarantyev makes off with the watch.)

**CURTAIN**

# ABOUT THE AUTHOR

**Frank J. Morlock** has written and translated many plays since retiring from the legal profession in 1992. His translations have also appeared on Project Gutenberg, the Alexandre Dumas Père web page, Literature in the Age of Napoléon, Infinite Artistries.com, and Munsey's (formerly Blackmask). In 2006 he received an award from the North American Jules Verne Society for his translations of Verne's plays. He lives and works in México.

www.ingramcontent.com/pod-product-compliance
Lightning Source LLC
LaVergne TN
LVHW041616070426
835507LV00008B/274